Teaching the Argument
in Writing

"Teaching the Argument in Writing"

Richard Fulkerson
East Texas State University

National Council of Teachers of English
1111 W. Kenyon Road, Urbana, Illinois 61801-1096

Excerpt from "The Birdman of Leavenworth" on p. 127, © 1984 Time Inc. Reprinted by permission.

Manuscript Editors: Robert A. Heister, David A. Hamburg
Humanities & Sciences Associates

Production Editor: Peter Feely

Interior Design: Doug Burnett

Cover Design: Jenny Jensen Greenleaf

NCTE Stock Number: 01909-3050

It is the policy of NCTE in its journals and other publications to provide a forum for the open discussion of ideas concerning the content and the teaching of English and the language arts. Publicity accorded to any particular point of view does not imply endorsement by the Executive Committee, the Board of Directors, or the membership at large, except in announcements of policy, where such endorsement is clearly specified.

Library of Congress Cataloging-in-Publication Data

Fulkerson, Richard.
    Teaching the argument in writing / Richard Fulkerson.
        p. cm.
    Includes bibliographical references and index.
    ISBN 0-8141-0190-9
        1. English language—Rhetoric—Study and teaching. 2. Persuasion
(Rhetoric)—Study and teaching. I. Title.
PE1404.F85 1996
808'.042'07—dc20   96-6295
                                                                   CIP

This work is for Sharon, who has argued with me for more than thirty years

Contents

Preface: To the Reader

I have written this monograph because I have a profound commitment to the importance of argument in a free society. As you will see, I endorse a broad view of argument, a view in which the purpose is not victory over an opponent but mutual dialectical interchange through which, out of opposing yet simultaneously cooperating voices, wise decisions can be reached, decisions always subject to revision as better arguments and better evidence become available.

Effective argumentation is not a natural human ability but must be learned. In general, it falls to English teachers, specifically writing teachers (as well as speech teachers), to show students how to argue. Yet little in the teachers' preparation has given them the perspective or background information that would help them teach argumentation effectively. To remedy that situation is the purpose of this book. I hope high school and college writing teachers come away from it both more committed to the teaching of argumentative writing and more confident about how to teach and respond to it.

Much of my personal life for the past four decades has seemed to be leading to the production of this text. I grew up in a family full of educators who were constantly arguing politics, educational theory, and the politics of education around the dinner table. During my junior year in high school, a speech teacher noticed my propensity to argue and suggested I try out for the debate team. So I had two years of not very effective high school debate. Then a college debate coach, to whom I am greatly indebted, took me under his wing and started to teach me about effective ethical argument. I was hooked and spent all of my free time working on intercollegiate debate.

Along the way, I met my wife, Sharon, to whom this volume is dedicated. She was first a friend, then a debate partner, then my coach, then a partner for life, and always my most severe critic.

Probably, it was, in part, my interest in argument that made me change majors after graduation from mathematics to English. But the effects of having studied mathematics and formal deductive proofs have stayed with me, even as I have rejected their applicability to real-world argumentation.

I taught composition, including argument, for seven years in graduate school, while I studied Victorian literature, often reading it as social and intellectual argumentation. I learned much about argument from Dickens, Carlyle, Mill, Arnold, and even Hardy. At the same time, I also worked with Edward P.J. Corbett and read *Classical Rhetoric for the Modern Student*—on my own, since, at the time, no English classes were devoted to rhetoric or composition.

Later I joined a Department of Literature and Languages, which included philosophy. I not only became something of a specialist in teaching the second-semester writing course, a course in argument, but also, eventually, had the opportunity to develop and teach the university general studies course in informal logic and critical thinking. Much of my work for this course shows up in this text. And I developed a graduate seminar in the teaching of argumentation that has been required of all our doctoral interns for the past fifteen years. Much earlier versions of this monograph were written for the students in that course. I greatly appreciate their tolerance and criticisms of various drafts of this work.

For ten years Sharon served as a city commissioner of Commerce, Texas, a position which required cooperative argument to win election and then cooperative argument to participate in decision making about such diverse matters as tax rates, incorporation of outlying areas, firings of city officials, utility rates, airport regulations, and the conduct of the city animal shelter. As her campaign manager and confidant, I heard—sometimes more than I wanted to—a lot about the ins and outs of making local government policies.

I have tried to make this text as specific as possible, using real example arguments and samples of student writing wherever possible. Since I have spent my career in one university and one small Texas town, these are the sources of my examples. I apologize to readers that they will hear a lot about Commerce and East Texas State University in these pages. But the argumentative examples I use are all drawn from life as I have lived it here for a quarter of a century. All the student writing is real and done by my own students.

Throughout this work, I assume that readers are already familiar with basic classroom procedures for teaching writing as an extended, complex, nonlinear process: prewriting heuristics, audience analysis, principles of effective classroom discussion, appropriate uses of models and modeling, and emphasis on extensive global revision in response to both teacher and peer commentary. None of this changes dramatically when the focus is on argumentation.

On the other hand, I assume readers who are not familiar with logic or argumentation theory. If, by chance, a specialist in argument or an informal logician gets hold of it, I hope it will be read charitably with the understanding that I am fully aware of the many issues relating to argument and informal logic that I have either finessed or treated loosely at best.

Finally, a word about theory and Theory. I hope readers who know modern discourse theory will recognize that this book is indeed informed by theory. However, I should be frank. I am not a fan of the various views collected under the umbrella of postmodernism. Yet variations on postmodernism and European theory seem to dominate composition scholarship right now. To postmodern readers, I suspect this book will seem hopelessly unenlightened. All I can say is that I do not see the arguments for postmodernism as convincing. Belief in its dominant premises seems to me largely an act of faith (or authority worship), and its nonfoundational epistemology works itself out in self-contradictory ways, as adherents declare absolutely (i.e., foundationally) that we can have no ground on which to build viewpoints and arguments because all viewpoints are discursive formations. So I will not be invoking, even tacitly, the names of Derrida, Foucault, Althusser, Lacan, Gramsci, Irigaray, Kristeva, or Fish.

Instead, the tacit theoretical bases for my work lie in the dialectical theory of Habermas, the hermeneutics of Heidegger, the new/old rhetoric of Chaim Perelman, the pragmatism of John Dewey, and the argument model of Stephen Toulmin, as well as the notion of the ongoing dialogue of the Burkean parlor. My debt to classical Aristotelian rhetoric will also be obvious. If my own theoretical orientation needs a label of some sort, I would choose the one Stephen Toulmin gave, not entirely in jest: neo-premodernism.

Since I intend this book as a practical contribution to classroom pedagogy and hope for a wide readership from professionals who are not necessarily enamored of theory (or Theory) in the abstract, I have kept "theory talk" to a minimum. Readers need not be familiar with the work of Habermas, Heidegger, and their like to follow my line of thought. And the needed terms and concepts from Toulmin are introduced and explained as used, so that no prior knowledge of Toulmin is necessary.

Introduction: Of Argument —A Dialogue

Cardius: I have heard it said, Paulus, that you regard all discourse as argument. Can that be true?

Paulus: I'm afraid I've been known to make such a rash remark, but when challenged, I back off from it—unless I'm pushed further, and then I maintain the position more extremely, partly by taking it as a metaphor.

Cardius: You have me confused but curious.

Paulus: Fine. Let me try to clarify. I'm sure you're familiar with the discourse classification scheme that appears in lots of textbooks and is sometimes summed up—usually derisively—as "EDNA"—exposition, description, narration, and argument.

Cardius: Yes, I've even taught from books organized that way. And I know there are lots of problems with EDNA, so I'm not defending it. But it does suggest that there may be some other sorts of writing than argument.

Paulus: Agreed. It does seem to say so. Now as far as I am concerned, EDNA is a nonlogical classification scheme to begin with. Supposedly, exposition and argument are defined by their purposes, to explain and to prove. But description and narration are defined quite differently, mainly by subject matter: description is writing about people, places, things from a spatial perspective, and narration tells events in time. My point is that one may describe for many different reasons—including to explain and argue—and one may narrate for many different reasons as well—including to explain and argue.

Cardius: Now we're getting somewhere. You've just used the words "explain" and "argue" in a pairing that suggested a difference between them. And if that is the case, then there must be some sort of discourse that isn't argument.

Paulus: Good point. Now let me make my argument against that position—even though we are having a dialogue that some people would not call an argument. When I used the two terms, I used them merely as reflecting ordinary usage in composition. I, in fact, maintain that what we teach as expository writing is argument.

Cardius: How so? (And I find that especially odd, seeing that you are director of a composition program in which the major difference between two required courses is that one is supposedly about exposition and the other, about argumentation.)

Paulus: Another very good point. Let me use it to make my position clear. You have, I take it, taught the course about exposition, correct?

Cardius: Sure have. Several times.

Paulus: And I assume that you taught your students a variety of different sorts of writing tasks, such as perhaps a comparison/contrast paper, or a how-to paper, maybe even an editorial, or a critical response to a text read in class.

Cardius: Well, we did some of that, but actually the course was more about personal-experience writing—such as "write about the last time you felt like an outsider" or "discuss the last time you were truly surprised and what it shows about yourself."

Paulus: Interesting assignments. I gather you are trying to produce future columnists. But let that pass. When your students wrote, did you ever suggest that their writing should have a thesis?

Cardius: Sometimes. Especially for the more standard assignments like the comparison paper. In fact, some of the better personal-experience papers also turned out to have a thesis, some sort of moral or insight that the paper all added up to.

Paulus: Great. That's my point.

Cardius: You've lost me. Just like the Romans in Cicero, you've gotten off the topic, which was—let me remind you—about whether all discourse is argument.

Paulus: Well, I haven't really left the topic, but I do have to make the connection between what I've just said and the point. By argument, I mean any sequence of assertions in which some are presented as the reasons or grounds for believing the others. For instance, if you say that "Johnny stole the copy card," you are likely immediately to add, "I know it because I saw him do it." Your first statement is the one you want me to accept or believe, and you offer the second one to back it up. If you just gave the first one, the chances are good that someone would ask why you thought so.

Cardius: OK, I'm familiar with that concept of argument—claims and grounds, or premises and conclusions, or even evidence and inference. But what does that have to do with a student writing about the first time he spent the night in a jail in Mexico?

Paulus: Well, when you finished reading that paper, did he draw any conclusions?

Cardius: Not really. He just said it wasn't pleasant and he wouldn't want to go through it again.

Paulus: And did he show you that it wasn't pleasant?

Cardius: Actually, the first time he wrote it, he didn't, but the second time, after some class feedback, he really did. He added details about cockroaches in the food, the floor that was slick with spit, that sort of gross stuff.

Paulus: And were you convinced?

Cardius: Yeah, it seemed really believable.

Paulus: So his personal-experience narrative contained enough details of the experience to prove to you that it was unpleasant and he wouldn't want to let it happen again.

Cardius: Yep, it was effective.

Paulus: I would then argue that his paper was an argument, an argument supporting the not especially controversial point that nights in some Mexican jails can be unpleasant. Did he explain how he happened to end up there?

Cardius: Something about getting drunk in a bar, I think.

Paulus: So did the paper probably convince readers that it isn't a good idea to go to Mexico and get drunk in that way in that sort of a bar because it can lead to an unpleasant experience?

Cardius: Probably. OK, I'll grant that you can twist that sort of personal-experience narrative-plus-moral into an argument.

Paulus: Good. I'll take that as assent to my argument.

Cardius: I didn't say that. What about a personal narrative that doesn't have any moral? Let's say it's a vivid narrative of a single athletic experience. Something like what gets done in a different context in the Irving Shaw short story about the eighty-yard run.

Paulus: Aha! You're making my job harder. Am I to assume that this is a good piece of writing, a well-done personal narrative?

Cardius: Sure.

Paulus: One that, as we say, "holds the reader's interest"?

Cardius: If you like.

Paulus: What is it about the writing that keeps the reader's interest?

Cardius: It could be a lot of different things. The desire to know how a good story ends. Or maybe the desire to know what the experience was like, since the readers won't ever have it. Or even if they have had it, they'll get a sense of reinforcement, that that really is what it was like.

Paulus: Exactly my point.

Cardius: Huh?

Paulus: I maintain that every well-done story of that sort, whether it has an overt moral/thesis or not, also has a subtext that says, "Reader, this is what it's like to be a human in this situation."

Cardius: I think you're playing sophistic tricks now.

Paulus: Maybe. Suppose you read such an essay and ended up saying, "I just don't believe this piece. Even if it really happened to the writer, it just doesn't work in the writing."

Cardius: That's happened fairly often. But, then, so has the opposite. Sometimes I cry over students' well-narrated experiences. And sometimes I laugh with them.

Paulus: Right. Would it be fair to say that the papers you cried over, you found moving?

Cardius: Of course.

Paulus: And would you then say that in order to be moving, they had to be convincing?

Cardius: Whoa. I find much fiction moving, even though I know it to be fiction. So it isn't convincing in that way.

Paulus: We'll need to come back to that in a minute. Let's stay with the student piece based on experience. Could it move you if you didn't find it—let us say—believable?

Cardius: Probably not. If I didn't believe it—and I don't mean by that that I decide that it really happened that way; I suppose I'm saying if it lacks verisimilitude—then I wouldn't probably be moved enough to cry over it.

Paulus: So, to sum up, as Socrates sometimes did when things seemed to have gotten far out in left field, you would find the personal paper without thesis effective or moving only if it was convincing. I maintain that the student has presented you with an argument. First, an argument that "this really happened to me; here is my proof." Second, an argument that "this is the sort of human experience at which one should be moved to sympathy." And in the good ones, a third argument: "This is the nature of our condition as humans here on earth. This could happen to you also, and you could have these emotions."

Cardius: You sure do have to stretch to make that an argument. I thought you didn't believe in reader-response criticism.

Paulus: I don't in its more extreme forms. But, of course, I believe that readers bring information of their own to a text, and that reading involves making inferences. Actually, I am about literature pretty much where Matthew Arnold was: good literature is a criticism of life, it "tells me" something, it gives me a "viewpoint" to consider. I see what we usually call "theme" in a literary work as its "argumentative conclusion." (Of course, I don't want to be identified with Arnold's views about social class or what makes great literature.)

Cardius: Well, now, here I think I've got you—and you may turn out to be closer to Arnold's views than you want. First, I know that you read junk detective fiction. And I don't think you can maintain that it has a viewpoint to consider, or is offered as an Arnoldian criticism of life.

Paulus: Good point. I'm not sure how I can get out of it without having to maintain some very strained position just to win the argument—such as that reading Sharon McCone or Spenser novels teaches me something about heroism. I have made that argument about reading Hemingway, where it's getting harder to take seriously, but Spenser? Doesn't seem likely. I don't read detective fiction for wit and wisdom, or even for a worldview—although I acknowledge that in the collected novels of a good mystery writer, a single worldview of some sort is presented. Questions about morality and humanness and maintaining one's ideals do come up. But I have to admit, that isn't what I read them for.

Cardius: And how about postmodern fiction that doesn't make sense, that deliberately doesn't have a worldview or a theme at all?

Paulus: That's too easy. By its very structure, postmodern literature is making hundreds of different arguments about what it means to know, about whether there is order in the world, about whether art should be orderly and conventional or not, about how important "creativity" is, about what makes something worth reading, even about what it means to read. Of course, in that sense, postmodernist art is mainly about art, and I suspect that is why it is generally of interest only to scholars.

Cardius: Well, I suspect I agree with you on that one. But I believe I have won the point about schlock fiction. And I think if we had more time, I could force you to admit that other sorts of writing are not actually argument. I would bring up front-page news stories, the minutes of university meetings that you frequently write, the telephone book, the little sheet of instructions you got with the calculator you bought today, the list of ingredients on the side of the bottle of pain pills, maybe the invitation to dinner you got for the weekend.

Paulus: And I would probably admit that at least some of those make your point. On the other hand, I would then argue that each of them is written for a reader, that behind each of them is an author who wants to get a certain reaction, and that in a large sense the text must be such as to argue the reader into behaving appropriately. Front-page news stories are easy to show. All you have to do is take a write-up about the same event from a liberal paper, a conservative paper, and perhaps a scandal sheet. Compare them and you will see that each argues for a vision of reality by the words it uses and the details it includes: even by what it puts first. And, of course, the author of the invitation wants to argue you into coming (persuade you, if you wish). I suppose even the telephone book people want to convince you that this is a useful document and easy to use so that you will, in fact, use it rather than call information. But it's 11:30, and I have some student journals to read. So can I argue you into calling this off?

Cardius: Only if I get the last word and say that I'll bet some of those journals are not arguments either.

Paulus: You're probably right. At least I'm convinced by your argument. On the other hand, however, the major reason I sometimes exaggerate and say that all discourse is argument is a pedagogical one. Most of what students will need to write, both in school and later, really is argument or would be improved if they considered it to be argument. Think of the essay test answers they sometimes write that are mere "data dumps" and how much better the answers would be if they had a clear thesis and used the data to carry it out. Or think of the often-wretched researched papers they write that have the same trait, or the book review that is only summary, when the professor wants to see some "intellectual analysis." And finally, I maintain that if students learn to write that sort of argument regularly, they will have no trouble backing off and writing the sort of text that isn't essentially argumentative, such as a recipe, or even an epideictic introduction of a guest speaker. I guess I'm willing to lie—or, at least, exaggerate—for my pedagogical goals. This is why I find both classical and modern rhetoric so very relevant. But that is a subject for a different dialogue.

Cardius: So you did get the last word after all.

1 The Pervasiveness of Argument

In Erika Lindemann's *A Rhetoric for Writing Teachers*, one finds chapters entitled "What Do Teachers Need to Know about Rhetoric?" and "What Do Teachers Need to Know about Linguistics?" But there is no corresponding chapter entitled "What Do Teachers Need to Know about Argument?" Argument and its companion, logic, are also missing from other similar books, including David Foster's *A Primer for Writing Teachers*; Huff and Kline's *The Contemporary Writing Curriculum*; and Thomas Newkirk's edited collection, *Nuts and Bolts*. Furthermore, there is no section on argument (or logic) and composition in either of the two major bibliographical sourcebooks on composition, Tate's *Teaching Composition: Twelve Bibliographical Essays* and Moran and Lunsford's *Research in Composition and Rhetoric*.

One conclusion seems obvious. A knowledge of argument/logic and its relationship to composition is not regarded as significant for composition teachers. It isn't part of the pedagogical paradigm of our discipline.

I used to be sure that it should be. Now, however, my position is a little more complex. I am convinced that logic per se should not be part of what we teach, and in that sense, logic isn't appropriate for our *pedagogical* paradigm. But I am equally convinced that writing teachers need to understand it, because logic provides much of the theory for argumentative discourse, and argumentative discourse is central to what we are about. So logic might be called part of the *preparation* paradigm, and thus I think it, together with argument, belongs in books like those cited above. Argumentation itself is inevitably bound up in our teaching of writing; i.e., it's part of our pedagogical paradigm. As a consequence, it should be a significant part of our preparation paradigm—but it very rarely is.

And that's why I've written this book—so that composition teachers in both high school and college can become familiar with both logic and argument in a context that stresses their relevance to the teachers' needs. Why writing teachers need to know logic, it will take the whole book to show, but you deserve at least an initial overview. First, a definition: logic is simply the careful study of argument patterns with the aim of distinguishing those that are satisfactory from those that are not, or perhaps more realistically, distinguishing how satisfactory a given argument is. Since argument pervades writing, it makes sense that writing teachers should know argumentation in practical terms and logic in more theoretical terms.

Let me be precise here—the definition of "logic" just given does not refer only, or even primarily, to that rather dry, mechanical, and formalistic study that the term frequently refers to. You may have heard of the difference between formal and informal logic, and that, in philosophy departments, courses exist in both. This monograph will touch on some relatively simple formal logic (in Appendix B), just so you'll know what it deals with and looks like, but most formal logic has little application to ordinary discourse, for reasons I will discuss later. Thus most of this book will be about what is now called informal logic, an emerging field with its own books, articles, journals, conferences—and controversies.

You may be familiar with some composition books that include treatments of logic. Most mix a bastardized formal logic and some informal logic (such as logical fallacies). If you are familiar with logic through English textbooks, you have probably had occasions when it was clear that there was a serious lack of "fit" between what a textbook said and what your students wrote. I hope this study helps clarify both the connections between what textbooks say about logic and argument and the frequent discrepancies.

For more than a century, it was traditional to classify types of nonfictional prose into description, narration, exposition, and argumentation (the EDNA classification). That scheme has been deservedly under attack for several decades. One of its unfortunate effects is to restrict "argumentation" to a particular pigeonhole of discourse and thus to imply that description, narration, and the exposition that we generally claim to teach are devoid of argument. Not so.

Another definition: an argument is any set of two or more assertions in which one (or more) is claimed to offer support for another.

Suppose a student writes a paper on dormitory life and in one paragraph remarks, "I was surprised to find out how small dormitory rooms really are. Ours are only ten feet by eighteen feet for two people." Now that is certainly expository prose, but it is also technically argument. The first sentence makes several claims (one about size and one about being surprised), and the second, by giving the actual dimensions of a dorm room shared by two people, offers support for the claim that dorm rooms are small.

This imaginary passage is scarcely controversial. Most American readers would agree that a ten-by-eighteen-foot room shared by two people is small. We could easily accept that this is descriptive prose (the dimensions of the room certainly describe it) and expository prose (the reader gets information about the room). Nevertheless, the two claims plus the implied relationship between them make an argument.

This simple example also illustrates another worthwhile point about argument. In discourse, it would be easy enough to reverse the order of the two sentences and produce, "Our dorm rooms are eighteen feet by ten feet and shared by two students. I was surprised to find out how small they were." Rearranging the discourse in this way changes some of its rhetorical effects, but it does not change the nature of the argument. The sentence about dimensions still offers support for the claim about size. The order of presentation is a rhetorical matter; it does not affect the argument or the logic involved.

Some further definitions:

1. *Arguments are made up of propositions.* A proposition is any assertion. That isn't terribly clear, but the idea of a proposition is basically like the idea of a point in geometry. It can't be defined very well; you just have to understand it. Here is a behavioral test for whether a clause or a sentence is a proposition or not: if one person states the sentence and another responds, "I agree with you" or "I disagree with you," and if this response produces a coherent dialogue, then the first sentence is a proposition.

For example, suppose Paulus says, "Can you tell me how to find Pecan Street?" If Cardius responds, "I agree with you," we find that incoherent. Cardius's response is just not what Paulus's contribution has called for. *Questions* are not propositions. Neither are commands. If Paulus says, "Call me at 10:00 tomorrow," it doesn't make sense for Cardius to respond with "I disagree." That much is fairly clear and easy to follow. It isn't so simple to apply the test to some other sentences that Paulus might utter. For example, suppose he says, "I will be in class tomorrow." Does it make sense for Cardius to respond with "I disagree"? My intuition is that it doesn't, but I can imagine a context in which it might. If Cardius, having just arrested Paulus, is taking him from a classroom, and as they exit, Paulus yells to the class, "I will be in class tomorrow," it might make sense for Cardius to respond, "No you won't. You will be appearing before the judge." Or suppose that Cardius says, "I like pizza with jalapeño peppers." Does it make sense for Paulus to say, "I disagree"? We sometimes hear such a response, but probably what

Paulus means is that he (unlike Claudius) dislikes pizza with jalapeño peppers, or that one should not like it. It would be very rare for Paulus to mean what he seems to be saying, that he is disputing the accuracy of Cardius's words about Cardius's own preferences ("you don't, in fact, like pizza with jalapeño peppers").

In practice we rarely have much difficulty determining in context whether a given clause is a proposition, although we sometimes have trouble deciding just how many propositions a clause contains. Obviously, if Cardius asserts, "His firing was both unfair and illegal," two propositions are involved. And real arguments frequently involve many more.

2. *Every argument involves at least two propositions.* A proposition that is offered as being supported by another proposition is called the *conclusion* or *claim* of the argument. The proposition or propositions offered as support are called *premises.* (Alternately, they are called *backing, grounds, support, proof,* or even *evidence.*)

What I have just defined is actually the simplest argument possible, one proposition supported by another. Real arguments are almost never that simple. The simple argument is very much like the kernel sentence in transformational grammar. By using several simple arguments plus some combinatorial principles, one produces much more complex arguments. (One might then define logic as the grammar of argument.) Just as you can take any English sentence and break it down to show the kernel sentences it is built of, you can do the same with any complex argument. Often, in order to decide whether an argument is acceptable, we have to break it into its simple parts and test each part. Of course, this is an interpretive act, and as such it is subject to all the difficulties inherent in any interpretation of a text. Many nonliterary ("discursive") texts are just as complex to interpret as the poetry of T. S. Eliot. The U.S. Constitution is an obvious example. So are many laws. So is a great deal of literary criticism.

In common usage, the word *argument* has several related meanings. It can mean a simple discourse of one premise and one conclusion. Or it can mean a more complex discourse of several premises and one conclusion. Or it can mean a quite complex discourse with several premises and several conclusions—perhaps even one in which the same proposition plays the role of conclusion in relation to one proposition and the role of premise in relation to another. And, of course, the word can refer to a verbal battle between two or more people, a quarrel. Finally, it is sometimes used to refer to an ongoing set of discourses taking different positions about a common issue, as in a phrase like the "argument over abortion."

With those definitions in mind, it becomes easier to see how pervasive argument is in discourse. English teachers often tell students that nearly all good nonliterary discourse has a thesis, implied if not stated. The thesis is what gives the discourse unity, what holds it together. And then the teachers have to explain what traits make an effective thesis. The following sentences won't do:

1. I want to tell you about my trip to Greece.
2. The purpose of this paper is to describe my favorite place.
3. The United States is a better place to live than Russia.
4. College is more interesting than high school, and you have more homework.

From the perspective of argument, one can explain more clearly why these are not likely to work well as thesis statements. The first two are not propositions and thus can't be thesis statements (both are topics rather than claims about topics). The third is indeed a proposition, but it is both vague (*better* in what ways?) and huge. And the fourth is a pair of propositions that have no obvious relationship except that both are about the same topic, college.

It's clear that any discourse with a thesis is an argument in which the thesis is the argumentative conclusion. English teachers have to be careful about the word *conclusion.* In its argumentative sense it means one thing (the proposition being argued for), while in its rhetorical sense it means quite another (the material that comes last). Often, the argumentative conclusion comes first in a piece of discourse, but the rhetorical conclusion by definition comes last. Students are frequently perplexed if we say something like "start with your conclusion."

If any discourse with a thesis is an argument, then it becomes even more clear why the current-traditional (EDNA) paradigm of description, narration, exposition, and argumentation doesn't make sense. A good description often has a unifying thesis about the place or person being described: "The room looked like a tornado had hit it." In that case, the description is an argument and can be judged by the appropriate logical standards. Frequently, too, a narrative is told in order to make a point, such as a biblical parable, a medieval *exemplum,* or a student's narrative essay of the time she learned that "even brave people can be afraid." In each case, the narration is an argument. And, of course, if a piece of exposition has a thesis, then the exposition is argument. That is why I claim that argument pervades discourse.

But I don't mean that *all* discourse is argument. You might be able to defend such a position (as Paulus more or less does in my opening dialogue), but I don't think it is especially helpful. What are some common types of discourse that are not arguments? Shopping lists aren't. Directions for opening a box of cereal are not arguments. Front-page news accounts of single events are not supposed to be arguments, despite what Paulus says. (But here we have to be careful, for these accounts often *contain* arguments. For example, "Three pieces of evidence indicate Johnson's guilt, a fingerprint, a telephone number in his address book, and a blood stain on his shirt." That is an appropriate newsy sentence, but it is also an argument.) Most recipes are not arguments. Summaries of discourse are not arguments themselves. Book reports are not arguments (although book reviews are). Road signs are not arguments. Neither are laws and regulations. And some ads are not arguments, such as "Have a Coke." I'll leave it to you to decide whether "Shop now and save" and "Just do it" actually involve arguments.

Common instances of discourse that we should easily recognize as arguments include editorials, most letters to the editor, letters of recommendation, evaluative reports of all kinds, discussions of causes, literary criticism, advice columns, most scholarly discourse, committee reports, and most "essays." Most job-related writing involves argument, as the following anecdote from English professor A. M. Tibbetts suggests:

An Anecdote

About thirty years ago, I was a young engineer working on a variety of commercial projects and experiments. I was having difficulty with the required writing—memos, letters, short daily reports, sometimes longer reports on finished work. After bogging down on one piece of writing, I went to the department head with my tale of woe.

"Well," he said, "try thinking this way. Imagine that every piece you write is an argument that asks a reader to *believe* or *do* something. Or both. Your job is to convince the reader to believe what you want him to, to do what you suggest. Lead him by the hand through your report or letter. When you think he might stumble, stop and find out why, and where you went wrong—because *you* are responsible for keeping him on his feet."

I went away feeling that my mind had been rinsed out with uncommon good sense. (92)

Perhaps more to the point, most school writing is argument. Consider the following discussion of the question by a high school English teacher, who wrote the piece as a reading log while she was a doctoral student:

English 677
Journal 1
January 27, 1987
Gail Herman
Sulphur Springs High School

I agree with your assertion that argument pervades discourse. Even if the writing is not organized as straight out argument, argument may be inherent in the writing. I decided to think about some of the writing assignments my students have done this year and to consider whether the finished papers contained elements of argument. I found that in many cases they did.

One assignment was an essay on a novel. We read and discussed Steinbeck's *Of Mice and Men;* then we had a discussion on writing about literature. I gave the students four topics to pick from and they went to work. (It sounds like it all happened so quickly! It didn't.) One suggested topic was to discuss the dreams of different characters. We had discussed how the characters' dreams are all unrealistic, so I was disappointed that more students did not use this idea as their thesis. Instead, more often I got something like "The characters in *Of Mice and Men* all have dreams." I expected them to tie the dreams together, to say something *about* the dreams. Had they done so, they would have been putting forth an argument: the characters' dreams do not come true because they are unrealistic.

Another assignment was to write a critical review of a young adult novel. The students were to consider the book's strengths and weaknesses and arrive at an overall evaluation of it. Basically, they ended up arguing "This is a good book because . . ." or "This book is lacking in that. . . ." Since they were either recommending or not recommending a book, their explanation and discussion of the book constituted argument.

Yet another assignment was to write an essay on the topic "what a class ring means to me." This essay was for a contest sponsored by ArtCarved Class Rings. We discussed audience and decided that clearly what these people would want would be essays that in effect would persuade the readers to buy class rings. Thus, while "explaining" what a class ring meant to them, my students were really arguing that every student needs a class ring and here are all the reasons why.

Argument can even creep into autobiographical narratives. Since I stressed that these essays had to make a point about something (or be focused, as on fear or embarrassment), in many cases the point made or the lesson learned turned out to be an argument. For example, one girl wrote of a sudden illness that befell her sister and of the impact that this had on the family. She concluded that, since tragedy can strike suddenly, we should not take our families for granted. This is, of course, not an original insight but, it seems to me, it is an argument. Another essay about an auto accident constituted an argument for safer driving. Quite often argument finds its way into student journals as when students argue against school policies they don't like.

Clearly, teachers need to understand the basics of argument in order to be able to guide their students more effectively. It seems to me that this kind of critical thinking skill would also be very useful in helping students learn how to interpret literature. As a rule, students are not careful enough to ground their interpretations in the text. In our discussion of *Of Mice and Men,* I mentioned that in a teaching guide I had read that the boss beat Crooks whenever something went wrong. I asked the students if they had gotten this impression. We decided to look for evidence which might support this assertion. All we could find that pertained to this issue was Candy's statement that, because George and Lennie were late arriving at the ranch, the boss "give the stable buck hell." Candy goes on to say that "The boss gives him [Crooks] hell when he's mad." We decided that these statements, while they do not necessarily rule out physical abuse, may merely refer to verbal abuse. The statements do not indicate conclusively that Crooks is beaten.

Thus, critical thinking skills are important in both composition and literature. I guess what I have here in this journal is argument by example that argument pervades discourse. Also present is the idea that teachers must themselves be in control of critical thinking skills in order to guide their students in both writing and reading.

Gail is quite accurate here, and a similar piece could be written by teachers in other fields besides English. Gail is also correct that she has made an argument herself, specifically a substantiation argument (discussed in Chapter 6) developed by generalization from examples (discussed in Chapter 4).

Finally, books and monographs like this one are in large measure argument.

Above, I have frequently had to use phrases like "nonliterary prose" and "nonfiction discourse" because we tend to distinguish writing designed to create an artistic experience from other sorts of writing. I'm no longer sure who the "we" is in that sentence, since some scholars in English now want to emphasize the unity of all discourses so that there is no inherent and definable difference separating literature from nonliterature. Others see the literature/nonliterature distinction as an unfortunate binary, with literature being the obviously privileged term, a binary that needs to be deconstructed. But I, at least, think the distinction still makes sense (without any privileging of either segment). Naturally some blurry cases exist that seem to bridge both realms. *The Grapes of Wrath,* for instance, is clearly both literature and nonliterature. So are the essays of Thomas Carlyle and Martin Luther King Jr.

Anyway, when we do make the distinction, we commonly restrict the definition of argument (and exposition) to nonliterary works. It seems clear to me that a literary work can both contain arguments (made by characters such as the fallen angels in *Paradise Lost*) and *be* an argument for its theme. But saying that raises some really complicated problems for evaluation of argument since of necessity the premises asserted by a work of fiction are not "true." It is an interesting issue in advanced argumentation, but not within the purview of this book (see Walter Fisher and Richard Filloy, "Argument in Drama and Literature: An Exploration"). I will adopt the following restriction. For the remainder of this work, whenever I use terms like *prose,* or *discourse,* or *writing,* the reader may mentally supply the provision that I mean "nonliterary" or "discursive" works. I do this to avoid the question of whether literature can be argument rather than to settle it.

2 Approaches to the Study of Argument

Logic is often defined as "the systematic study of argument," but logic now comes in two different varieties: formal and informal. These terms are not unchallenged: To a "formal logician" there is no such thing as a logic that isn't formal. And to some informal logicians, formal logic is seen as essentially useless. Moreover, since informal logic is anything but casual, perhaps it should be "nonformal" (Stephen Toulmin's term is "substantive" logic).

Formal logic is the study of valid and invalid argument forms. The study goes back to Aristotle's *Prior* and *Posterior Analytics*. It has a long, interesting, and complex history, although it did not actually change much until early in the twentieth century (see Kneale and Kneale). Traditional formal logic was concerned specifically with the reasoning form known as the syllogism (which, for those who are interested, is discussed in some detail in Appendix B). The syllogism consists of two statements called premises, which share a common term and a prescribed grammatical structure (involving two nouns and a linking verb), plus a conclusion with that same grammatical structure. If the syllogism is formally correct, the truth of the two premises would guarantee the truth of the conclusion; it doesn't matter what specific content it has—at least it doesn't matter to a logician, who is concerned with validity, not substance. In the early twentieth century, Bertrand Russell introduced a new and much more complex version of formal logic in his and Alfred North Whitehead's *Principia Mathematica*, a sort of logic known as symbolic logic, which includes yet another sort called predicate logic. Neither of these is ever seen outside the pages of logic textbooks, math books, and a few books on the intricacies of computer programming, so they need not concern us here. Readers who are interested in symbolic logic, which looks more like algebra than anything else, may consult any of a number of textbooks, including the ancestor of all contemporary logic books, Irving Copi's *Introduction to Logic*, now in its ninth edition (with Carl Cohen).

It is fairly common for college writing textbooks to introduce some of the paraphernalia of traditional formal logic, usually an abbreviated (and misleading) discussion of the syllogism (see my "Technical Logic, Comp-Logic, and the Teaching of Writing"). I take the position that English teachers need to understand syllogistic reasoning, which is why I include Appendix B. But I also maintain they should not, repeat *not*, bring syllogisms and their attendant terms into the writing classroom. Doing so isn't useful, it is likely to be confusing, and it takes up a good deal of time. (That claim is also argued in Appendix B.)

Ever since Aristotle, it has also been traditional to distinguish deductive from inductive reasoning, with deductive reasoning being the only sort that can be reduced to formalisms. (So formal logicians actually study only deductive logic. They aren't concerned with induction, which they see as dubious reasoning based on messy substantive matters, argument in which even the truth of the premises doesn't guarantee the conclusion.)

Authors of composition textbooks often feel that they need to explain the deduction/induction distinction. Deduction *can* be distinguished from induction. But the distinction is both difficult and unnecessary, and English textbooks that make it generally do it badly, once more illustrating Pope's maxim about the dangers of "little knowledge":

> [*Scene:* a freshman composition class, meeting at an early period, say, 9 a.m. After checking the roll, collecting daily journals, answering a question or two, the teacher begins.]
>
> *Teacher:* OK, now what was the main subject of the reading assignment for today?
>
> *Class:* Induction and deduction.
>
> *Teacher:* Good. And what did your text say they were?
>
> *1st Student:* [Reading] "Inductive reasoning proceeds from a number of cases to a generalized conclusion: deductive reasoning proceeds from the application of a general principle to a particular case and then to a particular conclusion."
>
> *Teacher:* OK, that is *exactly* what it says. Now in your own words, what does that mean?
>
> *2nd Student:* It means that in induction you go from specific instances to a general conclusion, but in deduction you go from the general to the particular.
>
> *Teacher:* [Not sure of whether they understand or of how to find out without just stating it himself. Inspiration strikes, and he writes two brief paragraphs on the board.] OK, look at these paragraphs; this one starts by claiming that "Honors students are sometimes lazy." Then it develops with three examples. The second gives the same three examples, but puts the main point at the end: "Clearly, even honors students are sometimes lazy."

Class: Yeah, that's it. The first is deductive reasoning; the
second is inductive.

Teacher: That's what I suspected. You are confusing the *order* of
presentation of an argument with the *type* of reasoning. The
reasoning in these paragraphs is identical; both show
induction.

2nd Student: But that's what the book said! "Inductive reasoning proceeds from a number of particular cases to a generalized conclusion." That's what your second paragraph does,
but the first one is just the opposite. It *has* to be deduction.

The conversation continues, in circles mostly, for the rest of the
period. Ironically, the students have just reasoned very well from the
definition given in the textbook. They have applied the definition to the
teacher's sample paragraphs and come out with a conclusion, in almost
classical syllogistic form. The fact that the conclusion is wrong, though
validly derived, merely indicates the problems with the book's definition.

The teacher in our scene above is quite correct that, despite the
common use of the phrase "going from" in textbook definitions, the
order of presentation is irrelevant to the type of argument involved.
Whether one presents the premises first and follows with the conclusion or the conclusion first and follows with the premises (or some other
combination), the same set of premises and conclusions will always be
the same argument. That is one major difference between logical structure and rhetorical structure. Diagraming an argument (as explained in
Appendix A) can help solve this problem since it gets around the question of the order in which the discourse is presented.

But even if it is solved, other problems remain. The general-to-
specific distinction, for instance, can be anything but clear. Consider the
following argument as an example: "Most college students are in favor
of abortion rights, yet abortion rights are immoral, so colleges need to
offer courses in which the rights of the fetus are stressed." The word
"so" marks off the conclusion for us, and there are clearly two premises,
but which is more general, the premise "abortion rights are immoral"
or the claim "colleges need to offer courses in which the rights of the
fetus are stressed"? I suggest that the whole concept of general and specific is simply inapplicable here (the concepts may apply to noun categories, but not to propositions). If one is defining induction and deduction on the basis of generality and specificity of the premises and
claim, then neither definition fits this argument at all.

Furthermore, even logicians use the word "induction" in two
rather different senses. In sense one, induction means drawing a con-

clusion about a group of phenomena by examining a carefully chosen sample of the group and then generalizing from the sample. This is the sort of reasoning we are all familiar with from opinion polls and various statistical studies of causation. And it is probably what most of the English textbook authors have in mind when they define induction. But in sense two—the more important one in logic—"induction" refers to any argument in which the premises are offered as providing some reason to accept the conclusion but not as a guarantee. (It is only in this latter sense that the duality inductive/deductive takes in all of argumentation. If "induction" is used to mean "generalizing from a sample," then the induction/deduction pairing leaves no room for arguments by authority or arguments by sign, among others.)

For instance, suppose someone argued that "John is a senior, and the seniors are dismissed today to rehearse for graduation, so John is probably in the auditorium now." The adverbial hedge "probably" warns a reader: the arguer is not proposing that her premises guarantee her conclusion, but merely that they make it probable. To a logician, such an argument is inductive. Yet, since it moves from a general principle ("the seniors are all at rehearsal in the auditorium") to a specific application, it surely looks like a deductive argument—specifically, a syllogism—to many.

The following attempt to make the distinction, from Rorabacher's *Assignments in Exposition,* is typical:

> In induction we analyze particular instances to establish a general truth, but in deduction we begin with a general truth and from it "deduce," or derive, knowledge of a particular instance. Inductively, we progress from the parts to the whole; deductively, from the whole to the parts. (195)

If Rorabacher is defining *induction* and *deduction* as types of reasoning, as the context implies, then her analysis is inaccurately oversimple as explained above. But some teachers and texts have appropriated the terms *induction* and *deduction* to refer not to types of reasoning, but to *orders* of presenting material. Thus a block of discourse that begins with its point and then provides supporting detail is called "deductively ordered," and the same block with the point moved to the end becomes "inductively ordered." Nothing is inherently wrong with this usage. In fact, Fahnestock and Secor have said,

> Here perhaps is the only legitimate use of the terms "inductive" and "deductive" in written argument. They can be used to describe the organization of arguments, the deductive setting out the thesis at the beginning and the inductive disclosing it at the end. ("Teaching Argument" 30)

Using the terms to refer to patterns of presentation rather than to the type of argument presented is perhaps theoretically acceptable, but it is more than a little confusing to students and teachers alike.

A simple solution to these and other problems is not to use the terms "deduction" or "induction" at all. In teaching composition, one gains virtually nothing by them. Since deductive reasoning always requires a universal premise of some sort, and we live in a world of very few universals, students are almost never going to be reasoning deductively anyway. As Aristotle pointed out, the things we argue over are contingent matters. Even in his practical logic textbook, Michael Scriven, one of the leaders of the informal logic movement, tells students,

> You don't need to memorize the terms "inductive" and "deductive"; we mention them only because you may run across them in some of your background reading. A slight juggling of the premises (by adding some unstated ones) and the conclusions can always convert an inductive argument into a deductive one without any essential loss of the "point of the argument," so the distinction isn't one you would want to build very much on; and, to make matters worse, some of the most respected professional logicians in the country today think there aren't any pure examples of deductive argument anyway. (34; also, see Weddle)

Four "Approaches" to Argumentation

So much for formal/deductive logic. Except for Appendix B, the rest of this monograph will discuss argumentation from a nonformal perspective—or from several nonformal perspectives. Basically, there are four common nonformal approaches to argumentation, and I intend to synthesize at least three of them.

(1) The classical rhetorical approach to argument will be familiar to most composition teachers. It stresses the use of argument to make decisions in a "democracy," especially decisions in law courts and in public forums. It emphasizes certain formulaic elements (which together make up the "classical oration"), and its key source is (once again) Aristotle, who gave us the still important distinction among ethos, pathos, and logos as modes of persuasion, and the much discussed enthymeme as a pattern of reasoning paired with the example. Only implicit in Aristotle, but developed at length by later classical rhetoricians, was the doctrine of stasis theory, which will be discussed in Chapter 5 and then used as a framework for Chapters 6, 7, and 8.

(2) Aristotle is also the origin of an indirect approach to argumentation, fallacy theory. In *On Sophistical Refutations*, Aristotle wrote the

first of a good many works in which various unfair (but often effective) argumentative moves were named and defined. To Aristotle, these were ways of arguing that smacked of sophistry. To this day, most introductory logic textbooks, and many composition books, both high school and college alike, include a longer or shorter list of fallacies, complete with elegant Latin names, definitions, and illustrations. This approach to argument is useful, but since it is negative, it is not terribly helpful by itself. It seems to presume that any argument lacking the identified fallacies is a good argument, which isn't true—any more than writing free from grammatical errors is good writing. I discuss fallacy theory at some length late in the monograph (Chapters 9 and 10).

(3) In 1958, British philosopher Stephen Toulmin, distressed over what he called the "crude muddle" of deduction and induction, proposed a system of analyzing all arguments that has become known as the Toulmin model. It has not been widely adopted in the field of logic, but soon found fertile ground in speech communication, where it came to dominate argument textbooks. During the past decade, it has also been integrated into a host of composition texts and occasionally hailed as a major breakthrough. The model itself is problematic in some senses, but it provides a useful set of terms for discussing various features of simple arguments. For that reason, I will both explain and critique the model in Chapter 3, and then use Toulmin's terminology where it is helpful in the rest of the study. (For a more elaborate discussion, see my "The Toulmin Model of Argument and the Teaching of Composition.")

(4) The newest theory of argumentation is the "pragma-dialectical" approach being developed at the University of Amsterdam by the leaders of the International Society for the Study of Argument (ISSA). This approach presumes that all argument goes on between two (or more) discussants who are engaged in a mutual, synchronous interaction aimed at resolving an issue. That is where the "dialectical" comes from. The approach also borrows from speech-act theory and linguistics the idea that all messages have semantic, syntactic, and pragmatic dimensions. And in this view, argument theory focuses on the pragmatic dimensions of argumentative messages, on what the messages do as acts, as much as what they assert. As an act, a message may request a definition, offer a definition, introduce evidence, retract an earlier statement, grant an opponent's proposition, etc. So far, most of the pragma-dialectical approach has been applied to finding exact conditions for describing with precision fallacious moves in simple and artificial argumentative dialogues. The system is relatively cumbersome and not without theoretical objections. Moreover, in large measure, it is an attempt

to systematize what argument analysts do more intuitively when they use a rhetorical approach and examine an argument within its context of audience and situation. It will not be used in the remainder of this monograph, partly because it seems, so far, to apply only to face-to-face oral exchanges, but those who are interested may consult Walton or any of the works of van Eemeren and Grootendorst.

In what follows, I shall argue that writing teachers need to know both syllogistic logic and fallacy theory but should not teach them. I will instead propose an adaptation of classical argumentation as the most fruitful approach to teaching students to write good arguments or to read argumentative texts effectively, and I will leave the classroom use of the Toulmin system as an open question.

A Philosophy of Argumentation

In Chapter 1, I distinguished among several meanings of "argument." Let me be more precise here. From now on, by an "argument" I mean a full discourse designed to establish a position by rational support (although not to the exclusion of pathos and ethos). An argument then is a textual product. It is composed of levels of sub-arguments going all the way down to specific factual evidence. By "argumentation" I will mean a process, either the internal process a writer goes through in constructing that text, a process in which she may well argue with herself before settling on a position, or the collective procedure in which a group of arguers interact in order to use their arguments to forge agreement among disparate voices.

As I perceive argumentation, it is the chief cognitive activity by which a democracy, a field of study, a corporation, or a committee functions. It is the overt sign of human rationality (see Billig's *Arguing and Thinking*). And it is vitally important that high school and college students learn both to argue well and to critique the arguments of others. In a postmodern world, what we call *knowledge* is the result of extended argumentation. Some of that argumentation is agonistic or adversarial—as when we have two lawyers or teams of lawyers make the best arguments for opposing positions. Unfortunately, this is probably the more common image our students come up with when told to write an argument. They participate in what Lakoff and Johnson have called one of the dominant metaphors of our culture, "argument-as-war" (4). They see an issue as two-sided, and the goal as presenting their own view in a way that will defeat their opponents.

But I want students to see argument in a larger, less militant, and more comprehensive context—one in which the goal is not victory but a good decision, one in which all arguers are at risk of needing to alter their views, one in which a participant takes seriously and fairly the views different from his or her own. If agonistic argument is displayed in the courtroom, the larger context I am suggesting (sometimes called *irenic*) is displayed in the jury room and by appellate judges. It is crucial that students learn to participate effectively in argumentation as a co-operative, dialectical exchange and a search for mutually acceptable (and contingent) answers, not just in English, and not just in schools. (See Crusius for a Heideggerian elaboration of this viewpoint.)

3 The Toulmin Model of Argument

In 1958 British philosopher Stephen Toulmin published *The Uses of Argument,* a scathing attack on traditional logic, in which he proposed what has since become known as the "Toulmin model of argument." According to Toulmin, the traditional distinctions between inductive and deductive arguments are "a crude muddle" (147). He also makes the more daring claim that canons of validity, instead of being universal traits of an argument's form, are agreed-upon conventions held by members of an argument field. Thus, to Toulmin, logical validity is field-dependent, a position that traditional logicians reject out of hand.

As Charles Kneupper points out, "Toulmin logic" soon replaced traditional discussion of induction, deduction, and the syllogism in most textbooks in speech. And it has been the subject of a number of articles by both speech scholars and logicians. "Toulmin logic," however, has not yet been widely adopted, or even attended to, in composition studies, but it is currently becoming a common feature in newer textbooks on argument and composition (see Hairston; Rottenberg; Ramage and Bean; and Barnet and Bedau).

According to Toulmin, all arguments, those traditionally called inductive as well as those called deductive, include the same general elements. All argument involves *"movement* from accepted *data,* through *warrant* to a *claim"* (Brockriede and Ehninger 242). The data are the facts cited as premises or support. The claim is the argument's conclusion, and the warrant is a general operating principle or rule of thumb allowing a bridge to be made between data and claim.

Brockriede and Ehninger, who have been largely responsible for the acceptance of Toulmin's theories in speech, offer an illustration of the three main elements of any argument (see Figure 1). The illustration in Figure 1 is an argument by generalization, based on an extremely large sample of past actions. The warrant is a variation of the essential principle underlying all generalizations that "what is true of a sample is true of the whole as well." (This will be discussed further in Chapter 4.) It's easy to see how a traditional syllogistic argument might also be mapped onto the model simply by restating the data as a minor premise, taking the warrant as a major premise, and thus taking the Toulmin claim as the conclusion.

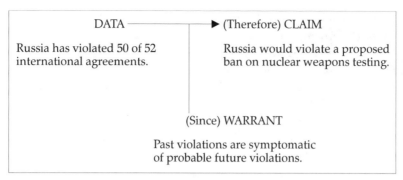

Figure 1. The core of the Toulmin model.

Toulmin's full model has three more parts to be added to the above diagram. Since most arguments lead to conclusions that are not *necessarily* true, but only *probably* so, Toulmin says a *qualifier* is needed in any argument. It is usually an adverbial hedge joined to the claim, indicating how strongly the arguer asserts that the warrant plus data support the claim. Various qualifiers are possible, ranging from "maybe" to "probably" to "almost certainly" to "must necessarily be the case."

Furthermore, Toulmin says that often the warrant, the principle by which one gets from data to claim, needs support itself. This support he calls *backing*.

Finally, the Toulmin model is completed by *reservations* (also called *rebuttals*), indicating the special conditions under which the data plus warrant might not lead to the conclusion. This portion of the model is illustrated most easily by using a legal example. Suppose we have facts showing that a student killed a professor. These are the data (also called *grounds* in Toulmin, Rieke, and Janik's textbook *An Introduction to Reasoning*). We also have a law that killing another person is murder. That law would act as a warrant. *Claim:* the student is guilty of murder. That illustrates the simple three-part version of Toulmin's model.

But if the situation is more complicated, the warrant may not be the law itself but precedent based on previous court cases defining what, for example, premeditation means. In that case we may have data plus warrant (legal precedent) plus backing for the warrant (specific previous court cases) plus a claim of guilty in the first degree. And even then, given the complex nature of juries and reality, we may qualify the conclusion with "probably" or "highly likely." Furthermore, we will be wise to acknowledge that the law also allows exceptions, so we will build into our presentation certain reservations such as "unless it is found that the student acted in self-defense or was temporarily insane." The schematic presentation in Figure 2 is now widely used to represent the full six-part Toulmin analysis.

The clearest and most thorough introduction to the Toulmin model is *An Introduction to Reasoning* by Toulmin, Rieke, and Janik. In that text, the material called "data" above is called *grounds,* and the "reservation" is called *rebuttal.* It isn't too hard to see how that substitution makes sense. The full argument in sentence form reads: "Given grounds G, and since warrant W because of backing B, therefore a properly (Q)ualified claim C holds, unless specific (R)ebuttals exist that cause the reasoning to fail."

The major goal of logic as the theory of argument is to sort arguments into two categories: roughly of the acceptable and the unacceptable or fallacious. So it is important to note that Toulmin's scheme does not directly include any principles of evaluation. It is not a normative system. In that sense, "Toulmin logic" is a misnomer, although it is entirely correct to talk about the "Toulmin model of argument." The six-part Toulmin model is essentially an analytical tool, not an evaluative one. The only way it could be used as an evaluation is by saying that since an argument is supposed to have six parts, an argument lacking any of them is defective. But Toulmin does not maintain that all six are needed in all cases. Backing for the warrant may not be necessary, for example. And warrants are often left unstated but nevertheless relied upon. If a pair of assertions qualifies as an argument at all (that is, if one is support for the other), then an assumed warrant can be "retrieved," and the argument can be cast in the Toulmin framework.

Suppose someone built the following argument using Toulmin's scheme:

WARRANT: All men are mortal.

DATA: Jean is a mortal.

BACKING: Throughout history, all known men have died.

QUALIFIER: It absolutely follows that,

REBUTTAL: Unless the laws of nature change,

CLAIM: Jean is a man.

Nothing about Toulmin's schema would allow one to say that the argument is unsatisfactory. It has all six needed parts. Of course, common sense and/or familiarity with syllogistic deduction reveals that the warrant plus data do not establish the claim, since the middle term ("mortals") is undistributed in both premises (Jean may be a pig). (See Appendix B for an explanation of what an *undistributed middle term* is.)

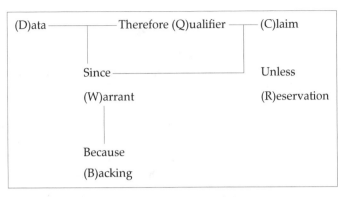

Figure 2. The complete Toulmin model.

Toulmin apparently assumes his readers understand certain fairly obvious principles of formal logic. So even in the Toulmin model, a sort of formal validity is needed.

For Toulmin, argument evaluation is finally field-dependent. That is, arguments are not judged good or bad on the basis of universal and timeless criteria, but are determined to be solid or defective on the basis of accepted standards of the field in which they are used. As Toulmin puts it, "all the *canons* for the criticism and assessment of arguments . . . are in practice field-dependent" (*Uses* 38; emphasis in original). And again, "the data we cite if a claim is challenged depend on the warrants we are prepared to operate with in that field" (*Uses* 100). "We must judge each field of substantial arguments by its own relevant standards" (*Uses* 234).

That is a far-reaching claim. It flies in the face of what logicians ordinarily mean by validity. And it makes arguments very hard to evaluate, for one must first be able to assign an argument to a specific field and then know that field well.

For arguments among specialists in scholarly fields, Toulmin's point makes eminent sense. I do not, for example, know the accepted methods for determining the composition of a distant star, so I am unable to criticize arguments about these components. However, I am confident that standards exist within the relevant fields by which knowledgeable people can distinguish a reasonable argument (even though it is not conclusive) from an obviously unacceptable one.

In practice, one learns to judge substantial arguments in all serious professions by "procedures . . . passed on from Master to Pupil in ways that *show* the differences between 'sound' procedures and 'shaky' ones" (Toulmin, "Logic and the Criticism of Arguments" 394). Toulmin illustrates with a law school professor who discusses at length the question of what constitutes admissible evidence (i.e., data), until the novices learn the canons of their business.

Toulmin's view of what makes an argument strong is not simple. It defies any attempt to cover "the principles" of good argument in an undergraduate course, be it in composition, rhetoric, or logic. And it is made more difficult when we ask just what makes up a field. (The question is parallel to the arguments in literary theory about what makes up an interpretive community or in contemporary rhetoric about discourse communities.) Is "English" a field? Or "composition studies"? What about "ethnographic composition studies"? Or consider "prehistoric extraterrestrial visitation," "creation science," or "deconstruction" (see Johnson, "Toulmin's Bold Experiment").

Among philosophers, not surprisingly, the model has essentially been rejected. Toulmin noted that his own doctoral adviser virtually refused to speak to him for twenty years after *The Uses of Argument* was published, and a colleague referred to it as Toulmin's antilogic book (Toulmin, "Logic and the Criticism of Arguments" 392).

But a number of scholars, especially those in speech, have found the scheme helpful for students. Kneupper asserts that it can be used as a generative heuristic for helping students construct arguments. They simply have to make sure they can fill in all six slots for a given argument. Of course, one argument's claim can become another argument's warrant, so that a chain of kernel arguments can become an extended argument and still fit within the Toulmin model.

William McCleary thought Toulmin's model might solve the problem of teaching practical argumentation in undergraduate writing courses. In an empirical study, some writing students were taught Toulmin, some were taught traditional syllogistic logic, and some were taught no logic at all. All groups wrote argumentative papers at the beginning and the end of the program. Unfortunately, the Toulmin students did not surpass the syllogistic group, and neither "logic" group wrote better arguments than the group who were taught no logic at all.

McCleary's study is revealing but not definitive. There are other ways of teaching Toulmin's views than the one he tried, and there are other ways of testing the outcome. But the findings are not surprising. Since, as discussed above, a good argument built around the Toulmin model requires at least an intuitive sense of how a syllogism works, as well as extensive knowledge of how reasoning is carried on in the relevant field, students taught the model largely by itself are not likely to construct effective arguments.

I have taught from several composition texts built partly on Toulmin's concepts (Gage, *The Shape of Reason;* Ramage and Bean, *Writing Arguments;* Rottenberg, *The Elements of Argument*), and my experience was consistent with McCleary's. My students had little trouble with the concepts of data and claim. But the idea of a warrant proved quite troublesome, as did the issue of how to provide backing for one.

One key problem with using Toulmin to help students produce effective argumentative discourse is the same as one with using traditional logic, the difficulty of getting from a model of a finished product to a process by which students can create one. Toulmin's model describes the argument as a product, but telling students their arguments must contain certain components and then pointing out those components in pieces of professional writing do not teach students *how* to create texts with those components. The heuristic possibilities of the model have not yet been carefully explored. (For a more extensive discussion, see my "The Toulmin Model of Argument and the Teaching of Composition.")

A second problem results from the stress on field dependence of arguments. Most argumentation taught in English or speech courses involves topics of general public or at least student interest rather than field-specific issues. If a student writes about problems in the operation of the university library, in what "field" of inquiry does the writing exist? Surely not library science, or even education. What about a paper in which a student argues for the value of living wills? A third problem is the question of whether the Toulmin model operates globally to describe entire discourses, or only locally to describe single kernel arguments, as Kneupper asserted when choosing to analyze only two paragraphs of Thoreau.

Toulmin's scheme can, however, be turned into an analytical tool for studying existing arguments by examining a text and looking for the claims plus the five supporting elements. This has been shown in a number of studies, including Kneupper's.

Jimmy Trent, in his doctoral dissertation, examined a large body of courtroom argument, using in part the Toulmin model. In these arguments, Trent found none whose claims were qualified, even though the premises would have warranted only qualified, not absolute, conclusions. Trent's findings are not surprising. In the triadic situation of a courtroom, lawyers are not expected to assert their claims with qualifiers or rebuttals. Those features of the argument are provided by the dialectic interplay of prosecution and defense.

A more interesting study is Roderick Hart's analysis of fifty-four persuasive speeches. He applied Toulmin macroscopically to entire pieces of discourse and concluded that "the amount of commonality a speaker perceives [with the audience] will affect the claims he makes, the data he offers, and the warrants he provides" (83). More specifically, Hart found "pronounced differences in the numbers of warrants explicitly supplied by speakers facing committed audiences and those facing collective distrust or disagreement" (84). Speakers facing hostile audiences used an average of two explicit warrants for each data-claim move, and "each warrant was stated, on the average, almost four times" (89). Generally, speakers facing already committed audiences neglected to supply warrants at all.

Given the difficulty of laying out real discourses in ways that reliably identify warrants as opposed to data and backing, however, one should be cautious about trusting such figures. Since few arguments are tidily laid out in the six-part scheme, we have much the same problem as in using traditional logic: the analyst must engage in considerable translation to see how the argument fits.

And a good deal of creative judgment is sometimes required. Peter Manicas pointed out that it is impossible to fit even the following simple and obviously valid argument into Toulmin's model:

> If I go to my first class tomorrow, I must get up very early and if I go to the party tonight, I will stay up very late. If I have to stay up very late and get up very early, I will have to get along on very little sleep. I can't get along on very little sleep; so I must either miss my first class tomorrow or stay away from the party tonight. (88)

Kandy Stroud's *Newsweek* "My Turn" column about pornographic rock lyrics may be a useful test case here. The entire text follows (with paragraph numbers added):

**Stop Pornographic Rock
by Kandy Stroud**

[1] My 15-year-old daughter unwittingly alerted me to the increasingly explicit nature of rock music. "You've got to hear this, Mom!" she insisted one afternoon, fast forwarding Prince's "Purple Rain" to the song "Darling Nikki." "But don't listen to the words," she added, an instant tip-off to pay attention. The beat was hard and pulsating, the music burlesque in feeling, as Prince, who has sold more than 9 million copies of "Purple Rain," began:

> *I knew a girl named Nikki*
> *I guess u could say she was a sex fiend*
> *I met her in a hotel lobby*
> *masturbating with a magazine*

[2] Unabashedly sexual lyrics like these, augmented by orgasmic moans and howls, compose the musical diet millions of children are now being fed at concerts, on albums, on radio and MTV. Rock stations may play Sheena Easton's latest hit, "Sugar Walls," as many as a dozen times a day. "I hate this song," my 13-year-old, rock-crazed son muttered on the way from school one day as he inadvertently tuned in Easton's lewd and crude song about genital arousal. My own Mr. Cool was visibly embarrassed. Embarrassed? I almost drove off the road.

[3] I confess to being something of a rock freak. I may be a singer of sacred music, but I've collected rock since its birth in the '50s. I've danced to it and now I do aerobics to it; I love the beat and the sound. But as both parent and musician I am concerned about the number of hit tunes that can only be called porn rock, and about the tasteless, graphic and gratuitous sexuality saturating the airwaves and filtering into our homes.

[4] Which is not to say rock took an erotic turn overnight. Elvis Presley was bumping and grinding his way through "Heartbreak Hotel" 30 years ago. "I Can't Get No Satisfaction," by the Rolling Stones, was no innocent ditty. But innuendo has given way to the overt. And vulgar lyrics supported by uncomfortably provocative sound effects result in musical pornography.

[5] "Feels so good inside," squeals Madonna on her triple-platinum album, "Like a Virgin." Rock's latest "it" girl hardly touts virginal innocence, as one can gather from her gyrations and undulations on Friday-night video shows.

[6] "Relax when you want to come," the English group Frankie Goes to Hollywood wails on "Relax," now the fourth-best-selling record in British history, a lofty position that being banned by the BBC did much to ensure. On the album "Defenders of the Faith," the group Judas Priest sings "Eat Me Alive," which deals with a girl being forced to commit oral sex at gunpoint. In "Ten Seconds to Love," Mötley Crüe croons about intercourse on an elevator. In concert, W.A.S.P.'s lead singer, Blackie Lawless, has appeared onstage wearing a codpiece with a buzz-saw blade between his thighs. During "The Torture Never Stops," Lawless pretends to pummel a woman dressed in a G-string and black hood, and, as fake blood cascades from the hood, he attacks her with the blade.

[7] Aristotle said music has the power to form character. The Bach B-Minor Mass can be a link with the eternal. But while music can ennoble and inspire, it can also degrade. Some drug programs forbid teenage patients to attend rock concerts or even to sport the T shirts of rock groups. Some schools where smoking and drinking are prohibited have added rock music to the list of taboos. "At the very least," says Father James Connor, the pastor of Holy Trinity Church in Washington, D.C., "rock is turning sex into something casual. It's as if society is encouraging its youngsters to get sexually involved."

[8] Dr. Joseph Novello, director of a drug program in Washington, says one of the questions he asks his teenage patients is what kind of music they listen to. Whether it's satanic, sexual or drug-oriented—it tells him something about the child's state of mind. In like manner, he says, parents have an obligation to be aware of their children's musical

tastes and "if you take exception to the words, don't allow them to listen."

[9] Surprisingly, the majority of parents I've spoken to have expressed partial or total ignorance of the music their children are dancing to, doing homework to, falling asleep to. Most claim they don't listen to rock or can't understand the words if they do. They also admit that they don't want to add another item to the laundry list of things they already monitor—movies, books, magazines, parties, friends, homework.

[10] *DOLLARS:* Legislative action may be needed, or better yet, a measure of self-restraint. If distillers can voluntarily keep their products off the public airwaves, then the record industry can also curb porn rock—or, at the very least, make sure that kids under 17 are not allowed into sexually explicit concerts.

[11] And what about the musicians themselves? If 46 pop superstars can cooperate to raise millions of dollars for African famine relief with their hit "We Are the World," why can't musicians also ensure that America's own youth will be fed a diet of rock music that is not only good to dance to but healthy for their hearts and minds and souls as well? (15)

A critic trying to use the Toulmin scheme on the essay first confronts the question of whether to treat it macroscopically as one argument (using Hart's approach) or microscopically as a series of kernel arguments (as Kneupper recommends). And if it is a series, one must decide how many major kernels it includes. In theory, one could diagram the entire essay (as discussed in Appendix A), then count the number of conclusions, and finally analyze the argument for each one by Toulmin's scheme. But such a procedure is unwieldy at best. To me the essay can best be understood as a nested group of five sub-arguments, a view that comes from stasis theory (see Chapters 5–8), rather than from Toulmin or any traditional logic concepts.

As I see it, here is Stroud's first main argument:

CLAIM: A good deal of contemporary rock music is sexually explicit.

DATA: Cited lyrics or summarized lyrics from seven songs by star performers.

WARRANT: The general inductive one that what is true of a sample is true of a wider group as well.

BACKING: Common experience of writer and reader.

REBUTTAL: She is not saying this is true of all rock lyrics, just of a significant portion of them.

QUALIFIER: None needed beyond the reservation.

Her second argument is essentially one of definition:

CLAIM: A good deal of contemporary rock music is porno-
            graphic.

DATA: A good deal of contemporary rock music is sexu-
            ally explicit as well as "tasteless, graphic and gra-
            tuitous" and "vulgar." [Note that the previous claim
            now becomes the data for the next kernel.]

WARRANT: Tasteless, graphic, gratuitous, vulgar, sexual explic-
            itness is certainly included in what our society
            means by pornography.

BACKING: None given; Stroud apparently assumes the audi-
            ence agrees.

REBUTTAL: Same as above.

QUALIFIER: None given.

Her third claim is evaluative:

CLAIM: Pornographic rock lyrics are harmful.

DATA: The lyrics are degrading and embarrassing to her
            and her son; the lyrics promote casual sexual in-
            volvement among the young; Father James Connor
            and Dr. Joseph Novello oppose the lyrics.

WARRANT: The reactions of typical listeners can be generalized
            to show the reactions of other listeners; priests and
            directors of drug programs are authorities on the
            young.

BACKING: None is given about the authorities; presumably
            readers are to judge from their own reactions
            whether the lyrics are embarrassing.

REBUTTAL: None given.

QUALIFIER: None given.

If Stroud had more carefully analyzed the lyrics she quotes, she could
have perhaps built a stronger argument that they are specifically sexist
and degrading to women, seeming even to countenance violent rapes. I
have actually merged two separate lines of argumentation here, since
they both lead to the same claim. One is an argument from her personal
experience of being shocked by the lyrics. The other is an argument by
authority. Note that I have actually included warrants for both lines.

Stroud's fourth claim is a generalized recommendation:

CLAIM: Something should be done about pornographic rock
            lyrics.

DATA: These lyrics are harmful to the young.

WARRANT: Society generally has an obligation to protect the young from corrupting influences.

BACKING: None cited, but presumably other social phenomena such as X-rating movies and preventing liquor sales to the young could be cited.

REBUTTAL: None given.

QUALIFIER: None given.

The fifth claim involves the policy that Stroud proposes:

CLAIM: The record industry should police itself.

DATA: The cooperative efforts of rock musicians to raise money for African relief, and the liquor industry's treatment of media advertising.

WARRANT: If rock musicians and the liquor industry cooperate sometimes for the public good, then they can and should do so at other times.

BACKING: None given (and these warrants seem to call for support).

REBUTTAL: None given.

QUALIFIER: Perhaps legislation is needed instead.

The final question, as with any detailed explication, is whether applying the system yields insights worth having that would not be equally well revealed by other critical approaches. If one were teaching critical, argument analysis, the Toulmin model might lead students to probe the makeup of an argument in some depth without their first having to master a great many rules of logic. According to Toulmin, Rieke, and Janik, the students would still need to understand the major substantive fallacies, however.

But argument analysis is not the main goal of a composition course. We want students to be able to produce effective arguments. Whether understanding the Toulmin model can help achieve that goal is as yet an open question, one on which we need considerable research.

For my purposes in this monograph, however, the major concepts from the Toulmin model will help to clarify the analysis of both general strategies of argument in Chapter 4 and of the various argumentative *stases* in Chapters 5–8.

4 General Strategies of Argument

In some texts on nonformal logic, the acronym GASCAP is used to help students remember six types of argument strategies:

G—Argument for a *Generalization*

A—Argument from *Analogy*

S —Argument from *Sign*

C—Causal Argument

A—Argument from *Authority*

P —Argument from *Principle*

These are major types of relationships possible between premises and claims in single argumentative steps (kernel arguments). But each can be used in larger patterns, either as sub-arguments or as broad frames; each can be diagramed (see Appendix A); each can be analyzed using the Toulmin model; each can be used both legitimately and fallaciously. In traditional logic, all are nondeductive arguments (with the possible exception of the argument from principle), because in each type, when well done, the claim follows only probably from the premises.

In a sense, the six GASCAP strategies play roles similar to what compositionists call *modes* of development—such as definition, comparison, and example. And the argument strategies bear the same relationship to the aims of argument that modes do to aims of discourse. The argument strategies, like the modes, are not ends in themselves but methods of achieving your argumentative end. Sometimes a single strategy is sufficient to make an argument, but more commonly (again, like the discourse modes), they work in combination. Nevertheless, for students in introductory logic classes, the strategies are often taught separately, partly to provide help in analyzing arguments and, more important, for help in evaluation, since each of the six has its own evaluative norms.

Several of these types of arguments, the ones I judge most important to (or the most complicated for) students, will be treated at more length in Chapter 6, but it will be just as well to give an overview of all six here. If each is analyzed as a full argument, then they can all be put into the basic Toulmin formula with a general and usually unstated warranting premise that justifies the entire strategy.

1. Argument for a Generalization

WARRANT: Whatever is true of a well-chosen sample will be true of the population it was selected from.

DATA: The sample has trait X, and the sample is chosen or constructed in such a way as to be typical.

CLAIM: Therefore, the larger group also has trait X.

Examples: All sorts of polls. Television Nielsen ratings. Generalizations about universities based on short visits, or about people based on first meetings, or about groups (such as student writers) based on sampling or case studies. Even reading an essay as a measure of writing skill involves generalizing from the document.

Uses: Generalizing may well be the most common form of reasoning. Whenever we meet people, we get a "sample" of their behavior and decide what we think about them. When we go to a restaurant, or leaf through a book, or listen to a politician for an hour, we are getting a sample. Quality control checks in industry involve sampling the product at intervals and generalizing to the whole. A scientific experiment is a sample of the behavior of elements of the universe; since we assume a uniformity in nature, a small sample (one experiment) is, in theory, logically sufficient.

Evaluation: Essentially by the STAR system. For a generalization to be reliable, we need a *S*ufficient number of *T*ypical, *A*ccurate, and *R*elevant instances. The poorer the sample, the more the claim needs to be qualified ("certainly," "very likely," "probably," "maybe," "possibly"). In professional polls, the criteria given in Ralph Johnson's "Poll-ution" are important, especially the margin of error.

2. Argument from Analogy

WARRANT: Two situations that are alike in most observable ways will tend to be alike in other ways also.

DATA: Facts about the observed similarities between the two cases.

CLAIM: Therefore, probably, they are also alike in some further feature.

Example: Many states with financial problems have adopted state lotteries. And the lotteries seem to raise a significant amount of money, without causing severe problems. Also, they are completely voluntary. Therefore, it's a good idea for Texas to adopt a lottery. (This argument was actually accepted by the citizens of Texas during the course of my writing this monograph. Note that the argument from analogy does not mean an argument by means of a metaphoric comparison. Logical analogies involve literally similar situations, which act as precedents for the situation at issue.)

Uses: Argument from analogy is used in law (Perelman and Olbrechts-Tyteca's "rule of justice" is that essentially similar cases must be treated in essentially similar ways; see *The New Rhetoric* 218–20), where precedent is crucial. Analogy is also used in deciding future policies (governmental, educational, institutional, etc.) if similar situations can be found in which the same policy is used somewhere else at present or was in the past. In science, analogy is used as a method of generating hypotheses to be tested but isn't a method of proof.

Evaluation: An analogy is made stronger by a greater number of *relevant* similarities, and it is weakened by dissimilarities that seem relevant to the claim. Of course, deciding what makes a similarity relevant or how seriously a dissimilarity weakens an analogy are interpretive activities based on experience, insight, and intuition; they are not algorithmic, or even rule governed.

3. Argument from Sign

> WARRANT: X can be taken as a sign that Y (which is not directly observable for some reason) is the case.
>
> DATA: X (the sign) is the case.
>
> CLAIM: Therefore, Y is probably true.

Example #1: When we stopped the driver, we had seen his car weaving from side to side on the highway. He was unable to walk a straight line, and he failed a Breathalyzer™ test. From these signs we concluded that he was legally intoxicated.

Example #2: We have a letter from a prospective job applicant which opens, "Dear Sir." He also uses the word "he" to refer to an assistant he hopes to hire. And he says that he "always believe(s) in hiring the best man for the job." Such use of male pronouns is sexist language, a sign that he is not really in favor of marketplace equality for women.

Uses: We use argument by sign whenever the matter at issue is a question of fact but not directly observable. Usually, the warrant for an argument from sign is based on prior reasoning by generalization: "In our past sample, X has been a sign of Y, so we conclude that it generally is such a sign, and therefore that it is a sign of Y in this case." A lie detector takes certain bodily signs as proof that one is lying. A doctor looks for typical signs of a disease to begin her diagnosis. An expert tracker looks for signs of the beasts he is after. Body language is often taken to be a sign that can be read by someone with experience. Other people believe that handwriting is such a sign. We take high ACT and SAT scores as signs that a student will do well in college. Scientists use signs of phenomena that can't be observed directly, such as the spectrum of light coming from a distant star in order to infer what elements are in the star. English scholars working in cultural studies use television, film, advertising, literature, and pop-culture phenomena as signs of our basic belief systems or ideologies. (Note: In everyday language, we might call this *reasoning by clues.*)

Evaluation: Judging the argument depends purely on how strong the relationship is between the overt sign (the clue) and the inferred claim. That is, is it always true that a fever indicates a virus? If it were, this would be an *infallible* sign; but since it is possible to have a fever and not a virus, it is actually a *fallible* sign (the distinction goes back to Aristotle). Does rough idling and dying at intersections always show a car to have a carburetor problem? Does everyone who fails a breath analysis have to be drunk? Will a student who scores high on the Daly Test of Writing Apprehension actually have trouble turning in high-quality writing on time? Criticizing such an argument usually involves explaining other ways in which the same signs can be produced and thus showing that they are fallible.

Often the STAR system can also be used here. Are there a sufficient number of relevant signs? Is the situation typical of the times the relationship has held in the past? Is the sign actually present? How relevant is that sign to the claim?

4. Causal Argument

> WARRANT: If condition X and condition Y nearly always appear together, then they are causally related. (But we don't yet know the exact nature of the relation—maybe both are the result of some other factor.)
>
> DATA: In many instances X and Y have appeared together and X has come first.

CLAIM: X causes Y, unless (rebuttal condition) there is some third common factor.

Example: I had been waking up with a painful headache off and on for several weeks. I began to examine my behavior. I soon found that each night that I read for several hours before going to sleep, I woke up with a headache. But on other nights, when I watched TV, or cleaned the garage, or played ball, I didn't have a headache. I concluded that my morning headaches were probably being caused by some sort of eye-strain the night before.

Uses: Causal reasoning is probably the most complex of the various forms. Yet it is absolutely necessary. If we want to know how to solve a disease, we need to know its cause. If we want to get a car to run, we have to know what is causing it not to. If we want to know how to teach students, we have to find out what effects various classroom practices have on them. If we want to grow crops, if we want to help the economy, if we want to predict the weather, etc. Scientists are concerned with de-termining the causal laws of our universe, such as those governing com-bustion, chemical reactions, plant growth, and gravitational attraction.

Evaluation: The big danger is reasoning *post hoc, ergo propter hoc* (Latin for "after the fact, therefore because of the fact"). If after watching por-nographic films in a laboratory, 55 percent of college males said they would commit rape if they were sure they would not be caught, one might think the pornography caused the response. But we would also have to know what percentage of college males would say yes to the question without having watched any pornography. If the other per-centage is 55 percent, then no causal relationship is shown. On the other hand, if only 25 percent of the "control" group answers yes, then by Mill's methods of agreement *and* difference (discussed in more detail in Chapter 6), some sort of causal connection has been shown. (But if the films the men watched also contained violence, then maybe it was the violence rather than the pornography that led to their answers.)

Other poor reasoning about causation includes claiming a partial cause is *the* cause, or the "real" cause ("the real causes of crime in our culture are poverty and ignorance"); failing to distinguish between proxi-mate causes and distant causes, or necessary and sufficient causes; or failing to realize that both phenomena are actually caused by a third. There is a well-known and strong correlation between ice-cream sales and crime rates: they go up and down together. But it isn't that ice cream causes crime—both are influenced by weather.

Again, the STAR system is relevant. If any sort of study has been done, then sufficient, typical, accurate, relevant information must have been gathered. If no study has been done, the reasoning is largely guesswork and should be carefully qualified with *maybe* or *possibly*.

In the hard sciences, some cause-and-effect connections are absolute and one-to-one. If you heat a metal rod and do not increase the pressure on it, it will expand. If you deprive a fire of oxygen, the fire will cease. But outside the laboratory, things are rarely that simple. Will an abused child always become an abusive parent? Will trying marijuana cause you to become an addict? (Does drinking milk lead to using drugs? After all, nearly every drug user started with milk.) Will arguing against a professor cause you to get a poor grade? Answer: it all depends. On what, we aren't sure.

One of the best examples in modern life concerns the causal link between cigarette smoking and lung cancer. It isn't an absolute one-to-one relationship, so the cigarette companies still contend that no causal connection has been "proved." But the evidence is so strong now that most informed people accept the connection, granting the claim that using tobacco significantly increases one's chances of developing lung cancer, just as drinking increases one's chances of having a wreck, and poor diet and overwork increase one's chances of becoming ill.

5. Argument from Authority

WARRANT: Whatever the expert says about X is probably correct.

BACKING: The expert has authoritative credentials on that subject.

DATA: The expert says that Y is the case.

CLAIM: Therefore, Y is true.

Example: My doctor says that I am suffering from bursitis, not a strained muscle. So I have bursitis (and should treat it accordingly).

Uses: Since we live in a complex world, it is impossible to know everything we need to know in making decisions. So when we have to decide many issues that we lack adequate personal knowledge of, we rely on experts: doctors, accountants, auto mechanics, writing teachers, economists.

Evaluation: The major question is whether X is a genuine authority (whatever that means) on the issue in question. Then, is it the sort of issue that all authorities are likely to agree on? If not, use STAR. Do a sufficient number of typical authorities, who are accurately cited and who have relevant credentials, all agree? Are there equally important authorities who say otherwise? If the weight of authoritative opinion is nearly all on one side, that side is *probably* correct. But then, at one time most authorities were sure the world was flat and that Galileo was wrong about planetary motion.

6. Argument from Principle

WARRANT: Principle X is generally regarded as true or proper.

DATA: This is the sort of situation to which that principle applies.

CLAIM: X is the case here.

Example #1: Since, in the U.S., we generally believe in "equality of opportunity," it is wrong to give college scholarships to high school debaters because not all students had the opportunity to be in debate. (Someone arguing for such scholarships would be likely to reason by analogy and say that debaters are, for this purpose, similar to athletes or band members who receive scholarships.)

Example #2: Since we generally believe in the right to privacy, I am not going to answer that question about my sex life as part of my election campaign.

Uses: Whenever we have to make value judgments, some general principle has been applied. Moreover, we often apply a previously identified causal connection in a predictive fashion: "Harsh criticisms of their writing generally turn students off, so if you really tell Randy that this essay is 'an absolute disaster,' he will probably just give up." The Toulmin model itself analyzes all arguments as forms of argument from principle, since the warrant is a statement of principle that applies to the data.

Evaluation: First, is the principle, in fact, generally accepted? Second, does it apply to the sort of situation in question? Third, are there commonly agreed on exceptions (such as one can take a human life if it is in self-defense)? Fourth, do other general principles lead to a different claim? Fifth, are the practical consequences of following the principle so obviously undesirable that we wish to alter the principle in the present case? Consider the principle that a child should live with its biological parents rather than its adoptive parents if the biological parents desire it. (We will return to this sort of argument in Chapter 7, under "claims of value.")

To what extent any of this material should be taught in a composition class is problematic. Certainly, it would be inappropriate to teach a given argument procedure and then assign students to write a paper illustrating it. That is a major confusion of ends and means. On the other hand, a student who understands the principles above is likely to be a better analytic reader of academic and other discourse, which is both of general value and helpful in using other texts in one's writing. Moreover, a student who is familiar with these principles may well be able to use them as criteria for revision within the context of an extended paper that joins several different types of argument, a topic I will discuss further in the next four chapters. This is another area in which classroom research is needed.

5 The Main Types of Claims: Lessons from Classical Rhetoric

In classical Greek and Roman rhetoric, the types of discourse were three: forensic (also called judicial), epideictic, and deliberative. Forensic discourse dealt with past events and the subjects of guilt or innocence; it was the argument of the courtroom. Epideictic dealt with the present and was largely ceremonial rhetoric praising heroes or (more rarely) blaming villains. Deliberative rhetoric dealt with the future and was the argument of the legislative process, focusing on consequences and expediency.

Within forensic rhetoric, *stasis*, or *status*, theory arose. If a person was charged with a crime, a number of different defenses could be used, and if he or she was to be found guilty of the crime, the prosecuting rhetor would have to show that three different questions could be answered in the affirmative.[1]

1. Did the accused commit the acts in question? A question of fact.
2. Do the acts in question constitute the crime charged? A question of definition.
3. Was the act such that no unique circumstances morally justified its commission? A question of values.

These questions are still relevant in a court, but if we join them with deliberative rhetoric, about what course of action should be followed, they can constitute the basis for a modern rhetorical system of classifying argumentative discourses, a system that is complete, useful, sequential, and elegant.

Stasis theory, unlike the induction/deduction pairing and unlike the GASCAP taxonomy, classifies arguments purely on the basis of what sort of assertion about reality is made in the major claim. Thus, it applies to full or extended arguments rather than to micro-arguments. In order to classify an argument as being within a stasis, all a reader has to do is locate the major claim and identify its type. Stasis theory is thus a classification of arguments by their purposes rather than by their strategies.

Several modern scholars have presented variations of classical stasis theory, and my own presentation—while somewhat different from any of them—owes much to their work. In a valuable rhetoric/reader in 1957, Harold Graves and Bernard Oldsey presented one version of modern stasis theory, although they did not refer to its classical origins. They stressed that each piece of writing could be thought of as answering a question and that the sequence of questions is

1. Questions of fact
2. Questions of definition
3. Questions of probability
4. Questions of value
5. Questions of policy

This sequence is very close to the classical progression, if we merge questions of fact with questions of probability. Whether the accused committed the acts is in one sense a question of fact: either the accused did or did not. But since we probably cannot know with certainty, it becomes—for argumentative purposes—a question of the likelihood or probability that the accused committed the acts in question.

More recently, Caroline Eckhardt and David Stewart have argued for a very similar "Functional Taxonomy of Composition." They note that our more common ways of classifying types of writing, either the Bainian categories of description, narration, exposition, and argumentation, or the common division into modes such as illustration, comparison-contrast, details, etc., stress *means* in discourse rather than ends. They propose that a more useful taxonomy can be built around the types of purposes one can have in writing. They thus divide essays into

1. Definition
2. Substantiation
3. Evaluation
4. Recommendation

Again we see the reformulation of classical rhetoric's stasis theory. In fact, the four can easily be applied directly to judicial discourse. Definition asks what are the components of the crime in question, say battery. Substantiation asks whether the accused probably (beyond a reasonable doubt in American jurisprudence) committed the acts. Evaluation asks whether she was somehow justified in her actions. And recommendation asks what should be done with her.

Eckhardt and Stewart, however, stress that these issues are not limited to judicial questions, but actually provide a comprehensive classification of the types of claims one can argue for. We can easily illustrate from almost any general topic, for example, affirmative action:

1. *Question of definition:* What is affirmative action, and how does it differ from and relate to equal employment opportunity?

2. *Question of substantiation:* Have colleges in the past five years made significant improvements in the hiring of minority faculty members?

3. *Question of evaluation:* Is reverse discrimination in hiring (or admission) policies justified by desires to encourage diversity in faculties and student bodies? Can nonminority faculty effectively teach courses in ethnic issues?

4. *Question of recommendation:* What sort of requirements and penalties should be placed on university athletic programs in order to achieve gender equity?

Eckhardt and Stewart stress that these are sequentially progressive, meaning that to answer a question of substantiation, you have to establish definitions. To evaluate, you will need both to define and substantiate. And to recommend that something be done, you must define, then substantiate, then evaluate the situation as less than acceptable, and then propose the recommendation to remedy the substantiated problem. That progression provides a sensible cumulative way to organize a course in argumentative writing, unlike taxonomies built on modes, which have no natural order and always turn out to be inherently but erratically overlapping.

Finally, Jeanne Fahnestock and Marie Secor, in several articles and a thoughtful textbook, have proposed a variation of the taxonomy. For them the types of thesis claims are

1. Categorical propositions ("X is Y")

2. Causal propositions ("X causes or results from Y")

3. Evaluative propositions ("X is Y" where Y is an evaluative category)

4. Proposals (which answer: "What should we do about X?")

Fahnestock and Secor give a good illustration of how the various stases showed up in the trial that grew out of the government investigation known as Abscam:

The first collision of charge and denial occurred at the stasis of fact: "You took the money" / "I did not take the money." Here the preponderance of evidence in the form of video tapes [*sic*] moved the issue to the stasis of definition: "You took a bribe"/"No, I took evidence for an investigation." As the bargaining proceeded, the defendants lost this issue, so the ground shifted to the third stasis of quality, where we can characterize the prosecution as maintaining: "You deserve censure for an act particularly reprehensible for a public official," and the defense mitigating this evaluation of the crime by answering: "I do not deserve such severe censure because I did not do what those who bribed me asked me to do." The final plea in the fourth stasis turns to the nature of the legal case itself and the jurisdiction of the court, the defense claiming entrapment and appealing to a higher court. Whether or not the investigation constituted entrapment is, of course, a question that takes us down to the stasis of definition again, and the two sides will continue to chase one another up and down the stases and in and out of the courts until the appeal process is exhausted. ("Toward a Modern Version of Stasis" 218)

Several newer argumentation texts also make extensive use of stasis theory, such as Ramage and Bean's *Writing Arguments;* Gage's *The Shape of Reason;* and Rottenberg's *Elements of Argument.*

These various schemes seem incredibly useful to me because they are non-overlapping and sequentially progressive, and as I hope to demonstrate in this and the next three chapters, they can serve as generative heuristics to help students create the arguments needed in a paper. Once students realize what sorts of theses they are attempting to support, then they also know a series of types of subordinate arguments which that sort of thesis requires in order to make a case that will persuade a critical reader. And these sub-arguments become heuristic questions causing the student to generate relevant information.

I'm going to modify the schemes to say that we need only three categories of thesis statement:

1. Substantiation—including
   - any needed definitions;
   - questions of fact if the facts are in doubt;
   - all categorical and comparative claims that do not involve value judgments (such as, "There are three and only three types of thesis statements that one can argue"); and
   - all causal statements that do not involve value judgments (such as, "The first-year class is getting smaller each year because of the rise of several new junior colleges in the region").

2. Evaluation—these include all claims asserting that something is good/bad, right/wrong, desirable/undesirable, valuable/worthless, moral/immoral, effective/ineffective. Such questions make up a large division of philosophy sometimes known as *axiology* (which includes both ethics and aesthetics).

3. Recommendation—these include all theses claiming that something should be done. Such claims are nearly always signaled by the word "should" or some synonym such as "ought" or "must."

In law and competitive debate, the term *prima facie* is used to describe an argumentative presentation that deals with all of the essential features demanded by the type of proposition being argued. A prima facie case is not necessarily a convincing one, but at least on first examination it is not obviously defective. Let me illustrate with a somewhat oversimplified example from American legal practice. In a civil court (as opposed to a criminal court) it is possible for one person to sue another for damages resulting from an assault. Technically, "assault" means "a harmful or offensive offer to touch another person which causes the other to fear such a touching is imminent. In addition, the touching must be unprivileged, unconsented, and not an act of self-defense" (adapted from Brand and White 178; also, see Josephson 10–11). In order for a plaintiff to recover damages for an assault, the plaintiff's lawyer must show that each of those conditions held, merely in order to present a prima facie case. If any feature of the case is lacking, the defense may move for dismissal, and the judge may throw the case out, the defense never needing to present any counterarguments. This is not to say that just because a prima facie case has been presented, the plaintiff will necessarily win the argument, but if the case presented is not prima facie, the plaintiff will necessarily lose.

I will maintain that each of the three types of stasis claims—substantiation, evaluation, recommendation—imposes different demands on the arguer for presenting a prima facie case. If students learn what the different requirements are, then these requirements can serve both as heuristics for discovering relevant support and as revision checklists for criticizing drafts. (They can also become critical-thinking probes for reading an argumentative text thoughtfully.)

A closing lesson from classical rhetoric: it became traditional to talk about the various parts of the classical oration, parts which supposedly existed whether the discourse was forensic, epideictic, or deliberative. Classical theorists disagreed over how many parts there were and about how rigid the form was, but a typical list includes

> Exordium—an introduction attracting the audience
>
> Narration—how the topic has come up at the moment; background to the issue
>
> Proposition—the claim to be argued for
>
> Confirmation—the premises upon which the claim rests
>
> Refutation—criticism of the arguments that would be advanced by someone arguing the opposing view
>
> Peroration—a moving conclusion

The classical orators recognized that the sorts of propositions that are worth arguing are almost never certain but nearly always contingent. Hence, the confirming arguments would never be absolutely solid, and premises would always be available to argue one or more opposing views. Thus, they explicitly built into their arguments a consideration of the opposition voices. That is an exceptionally wise strategy, one that too few of our students are able or willing to use. In fact, when I first discuss with students the need to include refutation, the typical reaction, even if the paper is based on research, is, "Why would I want to include arguments that weaken my own position?" That means my students are often willing to ignore research that conflicts with their claims and to assume that the reader will not know of it and thus will be convinced. They seem to think of argumentation and research as looking for material that supports conclusions they already believe rather than as a dialectical attempt to find answers. Such a view demeans argumentation.

I argue that such behavior is unethical. But assuming they are not likely to be persuaded by ethical principles, I further assert that ignoring the arguments against one's position is less persuasive than addressing them explicitly, conceding those one must (and raising ethos while doing it), and refuting the others (also enhancing ethos).

In a competitive debate (and other triadic situations), refutation is not part of a prima facie case because an opponent is expected to present the counterarguments, which can then be dealt with in later speeches. The same situation exists in the courtroom, where the prosecuting attorney is not expected to bring up defense arguments, since the defense attorney is charged with that task. Both of these rhetorical situations involve triadic communication in which side A deals with side B for the benefit of audience C. Here, the individual arguments presented by both (or several) sides are parts of the overall argumentation. But writing is usually not triadic. It is dyadic communication in which writer A has to address reader B and convince B of the soundness of A's position without immediate feedback from B or from opponents.[2]

I suggest that in all dyadic argumentation, no matter which stasis is involved, refutation of likely opposing arguments (especially those likely to come up in the mind of the reader) should be considered a part of the prima facie case.

Moreover, the goal of "refutation" should not be just to bring up opposing arguments in order to show that they are false. On complex issues, the opposition will surely have some solid arguments, that is, arguments that cannot be refuted. It is a good arguer's job to show that these arguments are understood and credited, but that they need not lead to rejecting the arguer's claim. Good reasons exist on both (or several) sides of questions worth arguing. And the purpose of argumentation in a free society or within a research field is to reach the best conclusion possible at the time.

6 Arguing Substantiation Claims

In one sense, the title of this chapter is nonsensical. Since all argument involves substantiating a claim, "arguing substantiation claims" is both redundant and all-inclusive. But as I noted in Chapter 4, I am using "substantiation" in a stipulated sense to mean all arguments of the first *stasis*, that is, arguments with claims that do not involve value judgments. In one sense or another, most of these claims can also be called descriptive generalizations (as opposed to evaluative generalizations), but that language would confuse this sort of claim with claims made by generalizing from a sample (as in GASCAP), which are only one type of substantiation claim. All six GASCAP modes can be used in substantiation arguments (as they can in evaluation and recommendation arguments). For explanatory purposes in the chapter, I am frequently going to refer to using examples as evidence for the substantiation claim. But readers should understand that the same principles apply *mutatis mutandis* to using authority, sign, analogy, or causal data.

The crucial question is, when is a substantiation argument fallacious and when is it credible? For composition teachers the question is not trivial. It is directly relevant to our students' writing, since what we ask for as a thesis is often a substantiation claim based on reading, direct experience, or observation. Moreover, the question of when a substantiation claim is adequately supported is relevant to what we say we know about teaching effectively, since our guidelines are themselves substantiation claims (causal ones), whether they rest on "experience" or on "research."[3]

The essential issues concern the quantity and quality of the evidence adduced for the claim. The most useful way I have found for deciding whether a substantiation claim is acceptably strong is to measure it against four ideal traits, traits which I sum up for students with the acronym STAR, introduced in the previous chapter.

> S—*Sufficiency of grounds:* Is there *enough* evidence to warrant the claim drawn?
>
> T—*Typicality:* Are the data representative of the group of data being argued about?
>
> A—*Accuracy:* Is the information used as data true?

R—*Relevance:* Is the claim asserted relevant to the information about the sample? (The warrant for the argument should supply the connection.)

Sufficiency of Grounds

It isn't easy to say how much evidence a sound substantiation argument requires. In fact, it depends on several different factors. If you bought a sealed bag of fifty individually wrapped caramels and found that the first three you unwrapped were brittle, almost crunchy, you would quickly conclude that the entire bag is probably brittle and crunchy. And that would be satisfactory reasoning.

Now suppose instead that you have a class of fifty history students, and you have each of them write an essay on what he or she knows about Prohibition in America. When you have read four papers of the fifty and found that all four show that students know little about Prohibition or have serious misconceptions about what life was like during the period, would you be willing to assert a claim about the whole group as you did with the caramels?

Probably not. The major difference is that one group is relatively homogeneous (we expect that all the caramels will be essentially alike) and the other is likely to be quite varied. In relative terms, it takes more data to adequately substantiate a claim about a varied target population than about a homogeneous one.

But the needed quantity of data also varies with the strength of the claim you wish to advance about the topic. Consider the fifty students again. After reading some of the papers and finding them uniformly lacking, you could conclude that

1. None of the students in my class knows anything at all about the Prohibition Era.

2. None of the students in my class knows much about the Prohibition Era.

3. A large majority of the students in my class knows very little about the Prohibition Era.

4. Most of the students in my class know very little about the Prohibition Era.

5. Quite a few of the students in my class know very little about Prohibition.

6. Some of my students know very little about Prohibition in America.

7. American college students know almost nothing about the Prohibition Era in America.

Claims one through six are arranged in order of decreasing strength. It would take a great deal of information about the class, probably even more than reading all fifty papers, to support the first claim. But the sixth one could be shown on the basis of only a few papers (provided that these papers actually demonstrate the writers' lack of knowledge). Number seven, however, generalizes to American college students on the basis of some students in one class at one university. Since we do not expect that "college students in America" are a particularly homogeneous group, such a claim is clearly not acceptable. The data are insufficient (and atypical as well).[4]

As a practical matter of rhetoric, the audience is also a relevant variable. A skeptical audience or one with little personal knowledge probably requires more evidence of a substantiation claim than a docile audience does or one that can supply relevant support from its own experiences. (Of course, a skeptical audience with lots of experiences that seem to contradict the claim being asserted will demand more evidence than an audience lacking that experience.)

And another practical matter of rhetoric, readability and extensiveness of evidence can be at odds. It's easy to cite two or three examples or two authorities or several signs to support a claim, but it's very difficult to keep a reader's attention through, say, ten examples or ten authorities. So the arguer must compromise, giving as much support as seems needed for the audience to accept the claim, hedging the claim if necessary, yet limiting the specific evidence to keep the piece readable, perhaps substituting statistical counts rather than specific examples or mentioning additional authorities in footnotes. (But these techniques also have problems.)

Typicality

If the data were perfectly typical of the subject being discussed, then the quantity of data wouldn't matter because the quality would be so good. If one caramel is like every other caramel, then sampling one is enough. That's why *Consumer Reports* can buy only one or two samples of a product, test them, and generalize about all the other instances of that product. So we cite more rather than less evidence, partly in order to increase the likelihood that our data are typical. But simply citing more evidence does no good if the principle upon which it is selected includes a bias in the first place.

Again, as a practical rhetorical matter, this criterion is difficult to satisfy in writing based on personal experience and observation. In several articles, I have made assertions about college composition textbooks and claimed that they frequently include inaccurate and misleading comments about syllogistic reasoning. Did every college composition textbook have an equal chance of getting into my discussion, or was there some bias in the selection? Obviously, the latter. I don't know every composition textbook and made no effort to compile a comprehensive list in the first place. Then did I select six books at random and discuss their treatment of syllogisms? No, of course not. Knowing that I was not presenting a typical sample, I chose to hedge my conclusion, claiming that many college textbooks (not all, not even most) contained serious errors. And I then tried to cite enough of them to justify "many," which was a stronger claim than "some." I also hoped that my audience would be familiar with some books and could supply further data from their experience.

When we argue from experience in our writing, the need for typicality should lead us to explain how we selected our data, to present it so that it shows no obvious bias to our reader, and to limit carefully the claim we draw from it. If a student wrote a paper about how hard college instructors were, and used three examples from the same discipline, any thoughtful readers should notice the atypicality. In revision, the student should notice it also, then decide whether to introduce further information about professors from other disciplines or to change the subject of the claim from college professors to college English professors (probably limited also to a single university).

One of the most famous, large-scale instances of a claim that proved unacceptable on the basis of its atypical data was the presidential poll conducted by the *Literary Digest* to predict the outcome of the 1936 election between Alf Landon and Franklin D. Roosevelt. The *Digest* had been taking a poll to predict presidential elections since 1916, and the poll had never been wrong in the five previous predictions. The *Digest* used a very large body of evidence. In the 1936 prediction, 2,375,000 ballots were returned. Sources disagree over how the sample was created and polled (Scriven says the polling was done over the telephone [*Reasoning* 201], but Newman says cards were mailed and returned [*Evidence* 207]). The large sample was taken at random from lists of people who owned automobiles and telephones (apparently, but sources disagree over this also). But in 1936, that excluded many people from even being considered for inclusion. In other words, by definition, the sample was not typical. That atypicality had not proved a problem in previous years, but in 1936, a much larger proportion of the relatively poor supported Roosevelt than was the case with the more affluent group the *Literary Digest* had polled. Newman claims that "the *Digest* was so discredited that it shortly ceased publication" (207).

In November of 1983, a local newspaper carried an article about a meeting of my hometown school board. Since I had a son still in high school, I was particularly interested—and probably read more carefully than usual. The lead sentence asserted, "College-bound Commerce High School seniors are accomplishing more in the classroom than their state and national counterparts, the Commerce Independent School District Board of Trustees learned Monday night." The article went on to give the support for this substantiation claim: "Seniors who graduated in May and participated in the Scholastic Aptitude Test had an average mean score of 475 points on verbal capabilities and 485 for mathematical capabilities." Verbally, this average was 63 points higher than statewide results and 50 points higher than the national mean. The local average math score was 32 points higher than the state average and 17 points higher than the national. Now the SAT has a standard error of about 20 points, so the 17-point victory over the national average for math may not be significant (it would not be significant if we were talking about a single student score, but for a group of scores it may be).

But if we apply the STAR test, we immediately see some problems. Was the evidence sufficient? Well, the target population, according to the lead, was "college-bound high school seniors at Commerce High." How large was the sample? We aren't told. Are we to assume that all the college-bound students took the SAT? That wouldn't be wise, especially since the article goes on to include some information about Commerce seniors who took the ACT. But we don't expect the sample for a generalization to include the whole target population. So the question to be asked is, "Was the group who took the SAT typical of college-bound Commerce seniors?" And the answer is probably no. In this part of the country at that time, the ACT was used more widely, and the only Commerce students likely to take the SAT were those considering going to prestige institutions that require the SAT. The more usual college-bound senior probably took the ACT.

And how did the seniors who took the ACT do? A brief paragraph notes that on the ACT, the students were below the mean scores on English, mathematics, social studies, and science. In other words, the college-bound seniors who took the ACT were below the mean scores on all four segments of that test. Nowhere in the presentation to the school board were the board members told how many students took each test. Yet the generalization drawn, at least by the reporter, claims the overall group of "college-bound seniors" is "accomplishing more in the classroom" than their national counterparts. Talk about accentuating the positive!

Accuracy

Obviously, if the facts used as evidence are not reported accurately, any argument based on them will be unsound. And equally obvious, it's virtually impossible for the reader of a presentation to know whether the data given are accurate. A number of rule-of-thumb principles have arisen over the years that tend to make some readers cautious about accepting "facts" under some conditions. Generally, we don't trust data when they are reported second- or thirdhand ("hearsay testimony"), since we suspect that messages degenerate in transmission and that inaccuracy creeps in as each sender selects from the previous message.

We don't trust statistics that are given as overly precise (such as a *Time* report in 1949 that the average Yale graduate of 1924 was then earning $25,111 a year; see Darrell Huff, *How to Lie with Statistics* 11). And we don't trust precise figures which are preceded with "It is estimated that . . ." or "Experts estimate. . . ."

We do trust eyewitness accounts, although a great deal of psychological research tells us that "seeing ought not to be believing" (see Norris and King), and we trust them even more if they are corroborated by different sources. We trust facts less when they are given by someone who somehow stands to profit from their being accepted (such as a school counselor presenting data about how well the students are doing) but more from a disinterested source.

For the writer trying to make a credible substantiation claim, all of the above dramatizes the need—while revising—to put yourself in the position of a critical reader. The reader is going to ask, "How do you know that factual assertion is accurate?" The writer needs to anticipate such a response and build into the discourse a mini-argument for the accuracy of the evidentiary claims.

Relevance

It seems obvious that the evidence upon which a substantiation claim rests has to be relevant to it. Yet, often, people give impressive data and then draw a claim from it that is connected in some way but not relevantly as conclusion and premise.

Suppose, for example, that a student presented a good deal of information about a course to show that the course is "irrelevant to success in my profession," then concluded, "Consequently, this course should not be required." There is an obvious shift between "irrelevant to my profession" and "not required," a shift that, in my experience at least, students often do not notice.

Or consider the following real student paragraph, written as a daily journal exercise in which the assignment was for students to make some sort of qualified generalization about the nature of students in their major field:

> A great number of students, especially women, majoring in some field of education do not plan to teach for longer than five years after graduation. Even though these students work to get an education degree, they do not plan to make teaching their life work. For example, a friend of mine who has been teaching math for three years has decided he no longer wants to teach school, but instead wants to go into some field of computer work. My roommate graduated last spring with a degree in elementary education. That summer she got married. Although she is teaching now, she plans to quit as soon as her husband graduates from school. My sister-in-law graduated four years ago in education, but she hasn't taught school yet. While she was in college, she had two children. Now she says she will start teaching as soon as the boys grow up. Still another friend of mine is a senior in social studies education. After she graduates this summer, she plans to get married and maybe will teach, but only until her husband graduates from law school. She has said to me that she does not want to teach, but is getting an education degree as a kind of insurance— something she can fall back on if anything should ever happen to her husband. This attitude seems to be prevalent among education majors. Students are using the education degree as a stepping stone to other fields or as insurance against future events, but very few of them plan to make teaching their life work.

Now in some ways, that is a good piece of writing—it is clear, well constructed, and developed extensively (in fact, it is so fully developed that we would probably tell the student it is too much for one paragraph). Notice, however, that the claim stated at both beginning and end of the paragraph makes an assertion about what education majors "plan" to do with their degrees. She has four supporting examples: her math friend, her roommate, her sister-in-law, and a second friend. Of the four, only the last actually shows an education major who at the time of the major did not "plan" to teach (she is getting the degree as insurance, but her plan is to be supported by her lawyer husband). The math teacher has apparently changed his mind after teaching for several years, but that doesn't show he did not plan to teach. And although the sister-in-law has not yet taught, she still plans to do so after her children are older. In other words, as now presented, three of the four examples are not relevant to the conclusion drawn from them (a conclusion which is stated much too strongly at the end of the paragraph). Probably, in revision, the bulk of the paragraph could be salvaged by modifying the claim, but if the claim is important to the author, then the supporting data need major modification.

Causal substantiation is important enough and complex enough to warrant some special discussion, although I have already discussed some of its difficulties as part of the GASCAP scheme in the previous chapter.

Causal reasoning is both one of the most natural and one of the most difficult sorts of reasoning. Humans naturally want to know what causes what, primarily, I think, so that they can control the outcomes by controlling the causes. Thus we always seek to find the cause of a given disease, or the cause of crime, or the cause of inflation, or the cause of certain behavioral patterns, such as homosexuality. We teachers of writing are always involved in cause/effect reasoning since we are trying to cause our students to write better. Hence, our arguments about the effectiveness of certain sorts of commentary on student papers, about whether studying formal grammar improves writing, about whether teaching students the five-paragraph essay has bad effects, and about whether sentence combining, freewriting, or peer review "works." All are questions about cause and effect.

Unfortunately, no human being can "observe" cause and effect. Cause and effect is a relationship between two situations, and at best we can see only the two situations and infer the causal connection. Often, the relationship is so complex and distant in time that determining what is causing what seems largely a matter of guesswork.

In fact, we can't even define what we mean by "cause" very clearly. Let's begin with what might be called the paradigm case, the idea of cause and effect in the hard sciences. In this case, we have two events that always occur together, and one either precedes the other or can be manipulated by the researcher. We know, for instance, that heating an iron bar causes the bar to expand. This is, as far as I know, an absolute cause-and-effect connection: every time the bar is heated, it gets larger. And if it gets smaller, we can be sure that it is colder.

There are many such connections in our world. If you remove the batteries, the flashlight will be caused not to turn on. If you heat the water long enough at a certain power level, it will boil. If you let loose of a pencil several feet above the ground, it will fall to earth. (Even some of these connections are less simple than they appear.)

We might call these situations examples of simple and proximate causation, "simple" because only one precondition and one outcome are involved, and "proximate" because there is no intervening chain of events. We should be aware, however, that many causal chains are more complicated than the idea of "proximate" cause: consider "the cause of death was massive bleeding, caused by a bullet wound to the heart, caused by a gun having been fired, caused by the sudden anger of the dead woman's husband, caused also by the existence of the gun in his closet, caused by the constitutional right to bear arms, caused by the authors of the U.S. constitution." So where do we assign cause?

Also, some further factors are often designated "contributing" causes that make life more complex. In the previous instance of the woman shot to death by her husband, we could consider the effects of his having drunk a lot of alcohol, of his having been fired from his job because of a government cutback, of their large debts for the medical care of a child, of his having discovered that she was about to divorce him, and of excessive ozone in the city atmosphere that day. Each of these might somehow have "contributed" to his actions and her death.

Sometimes the causal relationships can be clarified through the concepts of "necessary" cause and "sufficient" cause. In order for the woman to have been shot, it was "necessary" that the gun be available and that it be loaded. But, of course, the loaded gun may have been in their apartment for some time. By itself, the loaded gun doesn't cause the death. ("Guns don't kill people, people do," says the NRA.) But without the gun and the bullets, the death by gunshot could not have occurred; this makes the gun and bullets a necessary cause (sometimes called a background cause, or a contributing cause, or a predisposing cause). Which doesn't mean the husband would not have killed the wife without the presence of the gun. He might have used a knife or a baseball bat. Of course, if he had fired in a somewhat different direction, he might not have hit her, or might have only wounded her, so the actual direction of the shot also becomes a necessary cause. If it had been a small-caliber weapon, it might not have caused the massive bleeding. So the size of the bullet and the distance from which the shot was fired also become necessary parts of the overall package of cause and effect.

And this is a simple case, a case in which the necessary and even sufficient causes can be laid out fairly clearly, for this one instance, after the fact.

The more complex situations involve (1) general causal patterns that concern groups rather than individual cases, (2) complex mixtures of contributing causes in (3) situations in which not all the potentially relevant factors can be controlled or (4) the outcomes easily observed. As I indicated in the previous chapter, probably the best contemporary illustration is the long and complex research done on the effects of smoking on human health. Obviously, it isn't enough to say, "I have seen people smoke and then develop serious coughs and poor health." It isn't even enough to cite several people who smoked heavily and died of lung cancer before age sixty. And since we all know heavy smokers who live into their eighties and then die from causes that aren't apparently related to smoking, and since we also know that many people who neither smoke nor spend time around smokers die of lung cancer, we know that if smoking and lung cancer are related, it isn't by a simple one-to-one causation in which smoking is both necessary and sufficient to cause lung cancer.

For analyzing situations like these, we use complicated (and often unconvincing) statistical versions of Mill's "methods of causal reasoning" (for a fuller discussion of Mill's "methods," see Copi and Cohen, *Introduction to Logic* 9th ed., Chapter 12).

Let's begin with nonstatistical versions of Mill's methods. There are five of them.

Mill's Method of Agreement

If we have a series of different situations in which there is one common outcome (effect) and, in all the situations, there is one, and only one, common preexisting factor, we conclude that this factor must be the cause of the outcome. In this case, it is a sufficient cause. That explanation is too abstract to be useful, however. Imagine a case in which a circuit breaker in your house kept popping and shutting off the electricity. You might begin to keep records to figure out what was "causing" this to happen. If you also began finagling with your equipment in a quasi-scientific experiment, you might get the following data:

Case 1	Case 2	Case 3	Case 4
refrigerator off	refrigerator on	refrigerator off	refrigerator on
AC off	AC off	AC on	AC on
microwave on	microwave on	microwave on	microwave on
breaker pops	breaker pops	breaker pops	breaker pops

According to Mill's "method of agreement," if the breaker popping had always one, and only one, precondition, then that precondition is the cause (both necessary and sufficient) of the outcome. So given this set of data in this single instance, one would suspect that the microwave is causing the breaker to pop. Of course, this is a highly schematized situation. There are far more than three preconditions in a household, even if one restricts them to the sorts of conditions that past experience tells us are related to electrical circuitry.

And at this point, the systematic investigator would want to go further.

Mill's Method of Difference

In analyzing causation by the method of difference, we look for two almost identical situations that nevertheless had different outcomes. The situations must be identical, in fact, except for one factor. In everyday life, this most often occurs when we can alter that one factor at will. Suppose that an automobile will not start and has no lights. Then we install a new battery. Now the car starts and the lights turn on. It is the same car with the same motor, carburetor, gasoline, etc. Since the preconditions differ in only one respect, we are justified (more or less) in concluding that the battery is the cause of the car's failure to start.

To further test our theory, we might put the original battery back in. If the causal claim is correct, of course, the car will fail to start or to have lights. After doing this a couple of times, most people would be convinced that the old battery was the cause of the problem, a sufficient cause but obviously not a necessary one, since other conditions can cause the same problem.

It is the "method of difference" that is being attempted whenever we do studies in which we have a control group that is identical to an experimental group in all but one respect, namely the experimental treatment. If two writing classes are taught by identical procedures, with identical assignments and identical teachers, times of day, class size, etc., but one class does peer-group work and the other does not, then if the peer-group class writes better than the other, we are allowed to conclude by the method of difference that peer-group work caused the superior outcome. Needless to say, this is a description of a nonexistent "ideal experiment." In practice, no two classes are ever identical, no two identical teaching procedures exist, and something has to be done by the control group during the time the experimental group is practicing the peer workshopping.

Mill's Joint Method of Agreement and Difference

In the case of the circuit breaker above, the homeowner might well keep the microwave off for a couple of days and observe that the breaker stays on. Then she would use the microwave and (perhaps) observe that the breaker popped once again. This illustrates a use of the method of difference (the two instances of the breaker popping have only one different precondition).

But since the homeowner had already reached a causal theory by using the method of agreement, and now has further tested it with the method of difference, she has actually used the third method, the "joint method of agreement and difference."

Mill's Method of Concomitant Variation

Sometimes the preconditions and outcomes we are interested in do not occur in simple on/off states such as the starting of a car or the working of a circuit breaker. Sometimes they exist in measurable degrees, from zero through small results and on to larger ones. This situation is much easier to illustrate with group effects than with individual ones.

For instance, considerable research has been done on the survivors of the bombing of Nagasaki. Leukemia rates over the succeeding years have been accumulated for them, and the rates have been studied in relation to the distance the various survivors were from the epicenter of the bomb. And there is a high correlation: the survivors within two kilometers of the blast (about 30,000 people) died of leukemia at the rate of 9 per year from 1948 to 1955. Survivors who were more than 2 kilometers from the epicenter died at a much lower rate. Moreover, those within the 2-kilometer radius can be subdivided into bands and the likely radiation they received calculated: "The incidence of leukemia . . . is proportional to the estimated dose of radiation" (cited in Copi, *Introduction to Logic* 6th ed. 435).

This could, of course, be just startling coincidence, but to most rational minds, it strongly suggests that radiation from an atomic bomb blast contributes to causing leukemia. Obviously, this is not a sufficient cause, since not everyone at a given distance from the bomb blast develops leukemia, nor is it a necessary cause, since people contracted leukemia before there was an atomic bomb.

It is this sort of statistical, group analysis that has led us to conclude that tobacco smoking "contributes significantly" to lung cancer and other diseases. The causal relation is neither necessary nor sufficient, but we know that in groups of people who smoke in different amounts, from zero to ten cigarettes a day, to a pack a day, to two packs a day, the likelihood of developing lung cancer increases consistently. So the U.S. Surgeon General is convinced by the data, as are virtually all medical officials. But the American Tobacco Institute can point out that it is merely a statistical correlation and that most people who smoke heavily still don't die of lung cancer. Thus they can continue to deny the existence of a cause-and-effect relationship between their product and respiratory diseases. (And they can more strenuously deny the evidence of harmful effects from secondhand smoke.)

Mill's Method of Residues

This method is usable only in rare conditions, when a great deal is already known about a situation and where the outcome exists in varying degrees and as a consequence of several causes. The principle is that if there are only a specified number of preconditions, and several of them can be taken away, thus reducing the extent of the effect, then whatever effect remains is caused by the "residue" of factors. That makes no sense in the abstract, so let me illustrate it. I use it to weigh my dog, Mrs. Micawber. I already understand the causal principles of scales, gravity, and weight. I just can't get this dog to stand on a scale for me.

So I pick her up and stand on the scale myself, thus producing a reading (an effect of a certain measurable degree). Then I get back on the scale myself. I also produce a measurable effect. If I subtract my measurable effect from the effect of the two of us, the "method of residues" says that whatever effect is left over must be the result of the remaining cause. So here I can reason that the residue of poundage that I didn't cause was caused by Mrs. Micawber (in this case about 75 pounds).

Causal Argument and Teaching Writing

So what does all this have to do with teaching students to write arguments? The answer, unfortunately, is, not much. It isn't that students don't sometimes need to argue about cause and effect in their arguments. Both policy recommendation arguments and evaluation arguments sometimes depend crucially on causal substantiation claims. The problem is that it is rarely possible for a student to use any of Mill's methods to reason about cause. Most of the time, it is only possible when doing a library research paper and using the causal studies done by others. Even then, in real-world arguments, we get complex and conflicting data, such as those concerning the effects of capital punishment or the existence of gun-control laws on crime, or the effects of different systems of grading on student performance, or the effects of public school sex education on teen behavior.

All of this should make us cautious. It is a common assignment to ask students "to analyze the causes" of a particular situation or event they are familiar with. We may, for instance, ask them to discuss the reasons why they made a particular decision or to discuss the extent to which certain behaviors result from gender. Now some will write interesting and thoughtful papers about the pressures they felt; others will write what we regard as shallow papers. But the odds are that none of them is actually able to say much that could be tested by any of the principles of causal analysis. And since we "know" from a variety of psychological sources that human motives are complex things, not necessarily conscious, we should also realize that personal essays about why we did things are not likely to be very accurate. In fact, I suspect that in such essays what we are looking for is a narrative of what we teachers think self-awareness looks like, whether that narrative bears much relationship to reality or not. I have often been asked, for example, why it is that I switched major fields after graduating from college (from math to English). I don't know the reason—I'm not sure there are main reasons. But by discussing a number of possible psychological motives and their relative credibility to me, I can write an essay that would probably please most English teachers. Certainly, they are not in a position to dispute me, and I know enough not to make it look too simple and obvious.

I have also seen a somewhat less personal and more complex assignment, in which students are asked to gather data by interviews, and then by grouping the interviews, produce an "analysis" of the causes of a given phenomenon, such as "enrolling in 'Science Fiction,'" or "cheating on college tests," or "dropping out of college," or "not attending football games." Such papers can be interesting, even enlightening, but they don't really hold up as causal analysis. The paper presumes that the people interviewed (1) know what caused their behavior and (2) are willing to share it with the student writer. Both assumptions are problematic at best.

Most often, when students use causal reasoning in their papers, it is not the sort of reasoning identified by informal logic. In informal logic, causal reasoning means reasoning to a conclusion that is a statement of cause and effect. To do this nonfallaciously means somehow using one or more of Mill's methods. But causal reasoning most often plays a subordinate role in other sorts of argument, and when we need to know what effects a given plan of action may have, or what effects a certain behavior has, we are likely to turn to some authoritative source or some analogy or principle that sets up a "known" causal connection for us. Then, we use that causal connection and construct an argument from (causal) principle.

To illustrate: a student might be arguing against an increase in tuition and fees. And one of the arguments might be that the increase would cause a reduction in enrollment. There is no way to do a controlled study of the effects of tuition rates, but one can use the general causal principle that whenever the price of a commodity goes up, fewer people are likely to be able or willing to afford it, and thus build a respectable case for the idea that the increase might lead to loss of enrollment. Of course, the equally credible counterargument is that the increase is only a small percentage of the total cost, so raising it is hardly likely to make people who would otherwise pay tuition change their minds—another argument from causal principle.

My own judgment is that arguments of cause and effect almost have to be left to experts with lots of time, research skills, and money. The rest of us need to understand enough about causal reasoning to do a credible job of reading their studies critically. And that includes being able to compare studies with contradictory results and to withhold any judgment when necessary. It also means being properly skeptical of simple assertions of cause and effect, whether they be about economics, about crime, or about the effects of the newest fad in composition classrooms.

Cases in Point

Here, I want to illustrate what one can learn by applying the STAR system carefully to a piece of student writing. The piece I have chosen appeared in the East Texas State University student newspaper, *The East Texan,* on Friday, February 22, 1985. It is reproduced in full, below, with numbers added to the paragraphs to facilitate the discussion that follows:

[1] Since the times when wondering people put nickels into little black boxes just to see a few scratchy segments of moving film, the movie industry has been adopted by the American public.

[2] After the Nickelodeon, came silent films, then sound flicks, and then the *golden age of Hollywood.* That was really when movies were alive.

[3] During the golden age, it seemed that every new production was another gala attempt to advance, perfect and create. The movies from that period are to be savored and appreciated because they still live as works of art. But, their present day grandchildren hardly live up to those standards regarding actors, morals and subject matter.

[4] One of the main differences between old and new movies are the actors. Seasoned performers of old usually had a hard, long road to the top. But, for those who could reach stardom, the popularity was enor-

mous and lasting. A leading man, like Clark Gable, could expect to be a heart-throb for years.

[5] Today, the movie industry has turned to faces to fill their cast instead of talent. It's silly to think that just because a performer has a good body, or a nice smile, that they can act! Some of them have about as much personality as a cardboard box, but the blind public accepts them anyway.

[6] In truth, if one actor was substituted for another in a particular part today, who could tell the difference (unless it was one of the exceptional ones that do make movies worth watching)? But, let Cary Grant and Humphrey Bogart play a role, and their individuality shines through. They have a certain unforgettable quality that few have achieved in the industry today.

[7] Moral values have also changed in the movies. In the Golden Oldies, sex wasn't splashed on the screen for all to see. In most cases married couples had separate beds (remember William Powell and Myrna Loy in the "Thin Man" series). Even holding hands while sitting on a bed was taboo. True, that might be taking it to the extreme, but good movies were still produced without exploitation.

[8] Today's movies are just skin flicks where the first step after meeting someone is to hit the hay. With some of those scenes in recent movies, it's surprising that the film doesn't just sizzle.

[9] What about profanity? The world almost cracked when Gable said one word in "Gone With the Wind." But now, every other word rolling off an actor's lips is a new lesson in vulgarity. Have moral values really changed this much, or is the movie industry just trying to make us think that they have?

[10] Subject matter is another important factor. Early movies were usually based on literary works or seasoned plays. Today, it is as if the producers sit around saying, "Let's make a movie about ghosts and monsters with lots of blood, guts and gore," or "Let's make a movie about getting high." There just is not much substance there. Movies like "Casablanca," "The Maltese Falcon" and "The African Queen" will live forever in movie journals. But, honestly, how long will people remember "Eat My Dust" or "Friday the 13" (including all its sequels)? The answer is until another fast moving or bloody flick comes along to cheat the movie goer [*sic*] out of another $4.50.

[11] But, there is one saving grace for some new movies—technology. Back in the early days, Cagney had to dodge real bullets to get that effect. If he didn't do it right, it was too bad Jimmy. But today, it is possible to transport a viewer through space with a magic touch. Oh yes, there are some good new movies. "Star Wars" and "Raiders of the Lost Ark" both, among others, had excellent special effects.

[12] Just remember, if you are selective about what you go see at the theater, then you won't end up spending that money on a "B" movie that you wouldn't even go see on $1.50 night. And, if there is nothing worth seeing at the show, try working through all the mess on TV and finding a good old movie. There is a lot of talent and entertainment hiding behind the black and white. (4)

In many ways, this is a quite traditional piece of student writing. It is consistently built around a comparison-contrast structure, it has an explicit thesis stated early (in paragraph 3), and it makes three main points to support the thesis, each of which is forecast in the thesis.

Each of the three main points consists of a comparative evaluation of movies from the "golden age of Hollywood" with movies today, on one topic: the actors, the morals reflected, and the "subject matter." To make such arguments really requires several steps. A generalization about movies in the golden age must be made, then a companion generalization about today's movies. These generalizations must be different for the two target populations, and then an argument from principle must be made that the difference shows the inferiority of today's movies. Here, I'm more concerned with evaluating the generalizations than with evaluating the reasoning from principle used to make the evaluative comparison.

The first comparative claim is that the old films had better actors who took longer to reach stardom but then continued for years (paragraph 4). The instances cited are Clark Gable, Humphrey Bogart, and Cary Grant. Perhaps three examples might be sufficient for a single subpoint in a short paper. But their typicality can certainly be questioned. Obviously, they are all males, but the argument did not seem to be restricted to male stars (although the writer used the word *actor*, which she might intend in its gender-linked sense). Are these three typical of the actors of that period? Obviously not, but then that isn't what she is claiming. Are they typical of the stars of that age? Is it accurate to say that "their individuality shines through"? It seems so to me. No one would ever mistake Grant for Gable, even if they played the same role. And certainly their popularity was long-lasting.

Now what of the companion generalization about today's actors? In the first place, no examples are cited. The kindest thing one could say of the argument is that perhaps she expected that her college audience would provide the examples from their own experience. For the argument to be properly related to the previous one, it must deal with today's stars (c. 1984) and presumably show that they don't last long and/or aren't individuals in their performances. If critical readers think of Clint Eastwood or Paul Newman or Jack Nicholson, they might conclude that it's easy to give as much evidence about today's actors as she gave about those of the past. She gives herself an out, saying you can't tell today's actors apart "unless it was one of the exceptional ones that do make movies worth watching" (paragraph 6). Whether a star's individuality is necessary for a movie to be worth watching is arguable, but surely her own trio of Grant et al. were the "exceptional ones" of their day. To be fair, she needs to compare the leading names from today with the leading names from yesteryear, not the giants of the past with the un-named run-of-the-mill today.

When she reaches her second point (in paragraph 7), it is phrased as "moral values have also changed in the movies." That point is prob-ably undeniable, but it isn't an adequate subclaim, since she is going to assert not just difference but superiority for the golden age. She cites some examples of the lack of sexual explicitness permitted in older movies as well as the restrictions on profane/obscene language. It would be easy to cite specific contrasts from some current movies, but she doesn't do so. Again, she probably relies on her readers' familiarity with current movies. But in paragraph 8 she makes the extremely strong claim that "[t]oday's movies are just skin flicks where the first step after meet-ing someone is to hit the hay." Logically, it would take a complete count of every movie made to support such a universal claim, and one counterexample (such as *E.T.* or *Home Alone*) destroys it. A more gener-ous interpretation of what she intended would take her sentence to be hyperbole and assume her to mean something like "most of today's movies are skin flicks," a proposition for which she could cite a great deal of evidence but does not.

The argument about subject matter in paragraph 10 is interesting. She generalizes that early movies "were usually based on literary works or seasoned plays" and cites three examples: *Casablanca, The Maltese Fal-con*, and *The African Queen.* Obviously, three examples starring Bogart do not constitute a typical sample of movies of the age. I assume she is accurate in claiming that the three were based on another medium. But that, finally, isn't relevant. Her real point is that the quality of the sub-ject matter of older films is high in comparison with current films. Yet showing that films came from "literary works or seasoned plays" does not show quality content, unless she takes "literary works" in a special, privileged sense. (This is an argument by sign—being adapted from a different medium is a sign of quality subject matter in a movie.)

When she turns to modern movies, she does indeed cite several which have anything but great content, *Friday the 13th* and *Eat My Dust.* Are these two sufficient? Hardly. Are they typical? It doesn't seem likely. And if the issue is whether today's films come from "literary works or seasoned plays," it isn't hard to cite examples of modern movies (i.e., movies produced within a few years prior to the article's publication) based on books and plays: *The Right Stuff; One Flew Over the Cuckoo's Nest; The Last Picture Show; A Clockwork Orange; The Great Gatsby; An*

Officer and a Gentlemen; Sophie's Choice; and *The French Lieutenant's Woman* come to mind. These are not typical either, and I'm not sure they are relevant to the issue of "content quality," but they are relevant to determining whether the argument that movies of yesterday were based on literary originals while today's movies are not is sound.

My point is not to argue that the writer's position is wrong. I'm not a movie fan and have little personal knowledge of either side in this quarrel between ancients and moderns. My point is that student writers using evidence to make substantiation claims can be taught the standards for making them effectively and can thus improve the quality of their arguments. In order to teach them to improve such arguments, we composition teachers need, ourselves, to be aware of what makes a claim well grounded.

But let me close this chapter on substantiation arguments with a second piece of student writing, this one actually written as an assigned paper in a second-semester first-year writing class and thus, perhaps, more typical than a newspaper column. The class had read and discussed Deborah Tannen's *You Just Don't Understand* for several weeks, and the assignment asked students to relate or apply Tannen's views to discourse that they heard or participated in and to draw whatever conclusions seemed sensible, including possible critiques of Tannen:

Why Can't I Understand Him?
by Jonikka Page

"Why can't I understand him? We've been together two years, right? I should know him by now. We should be able to talk and understand what the other is trying to say without all the hurt feelings and mixed signals. What's wrong then? Is it that we're not right for each other?"

Late at night, I find myself in bed, wondering these same thoughts. Relentlessly, they creep through my mind. The sound of their approach grows louder and louder until I can't bear it anymore. They've come to threaten everything I dream about, everything that I want for the future. It's not too much to ask to have one person in your life to share things with and to be with. I found that person—Chris. I love him more than anything else in this world. We've been together for two years, and I've come to depend on him to be there to share my life with me. It seems so simple. Ideally, we would talk and share things—little things that no one else would care about:

> Chris: What did you do today? Did you have a good day?
>
> Jonikka: Not really. In band, David was talking about chair tests and he told Shelley that she could just take first chair since she was the only real flute player there.
>
> Chris: That sucks. I heard him say something like that. I looked up there to see what your reaction was, but I couldn't tell.

> That makes me mad! I'm going to tell Mr. Bennett about that. That's not fair.
>
> Jonikka: Do you think so, too? I sure am glad that I'm not the only one.

This conversation is one that is ideal as far as Deborah Tannen, *You Just Don't Understand,* says. The book is focused on the differences between the language that women use and the language that men use and their relationship to one another. She says that women's conversations are "negotiations for closeness in which people try to seek and give confirmation and support and to reach consensus" (Tannen 25). That is precisely why this conversation, to a woman, would seem like a dream come true. Chris agreed with me—"That sucks," "That's not fair,"—on this occasion and it brought us closer together. He supported me when I needed it.

This was not a typical, everyday conversation, though. I agree with Tannen in her consensus that "there are gender differences in ways of speaking, and we need to identify and understand them. Without such understanding, we are doomed to blame ourselves—or the relationship—for the otherwise mystifying and damaging effects of our contrasting conversational styles" (Tannen 17).

All humans need intimacy and independence, but it is generally true that women focus on the first and men on the latter. This can be exemplified in an example from Tannen's book. Josh invited an old friend who was going to be visiting in town to stay with him and Linda. He also had decided that he and Josh would go out the first night that the friend was in town. Linda was upset because Josh did not discuss his plans with her; he informed her of what was going to happen. Josh didn't understand this because he says that he could never tell his friend that he had to ask his wife for permission. This would "imply that he is not independent, not free to act on his own. It would make him feel like a child or an underling" (Tannen 26).

This is so familiar. Just recently, I have run into the same situation with Chris. It seems as if he has had a sudden need for freedom and a distinct fear of being seen by his friends as being a child reporting to me, his mother. This conversation shows his fear of having to seek permission from me for staying out and doing things with his friends:

> Jonikka: What are you going to do tonight?
>
> Chris: I'm going to practice for a while and then me and Garnett might go do something. So don't wait up. I don't know when we'll be finished so I'll just come up to your room whenever I get done.
>
> Jonikka: Well, okay. Just come whenever you get done I guess.
>
> Chris: I just don't want to have to call you. It makes me feel like you're my mother.

I was hurt because I felt that we discussed what we were going to do because what one of us did had consequences for the other. Not only did I not mind telling someone, "I have to check with Chris"; quite the contrary—I like it. Tannen says that it makes a woman feel good to know that she is involved with someone, "that her life is bound up with someone else's" (Tannen 27). Both of us ended up upset by the whole incident because it cuts to the core of our primary concerns. I was hurt because I sensed a failure of closeness in the relationship: He didn't care about me as much as I care about him. And he was hurt because he felt I was trying to control him and limit his freedom. Another incident tells of the same situation:

> Jonikka: Are you going to go to town this Saturday and go out with me on Friday or vice versa? (He usually goes out with his friends back home one night and me the other.)
> Chris: I don't know yet (slightly emphatically). I'll call you from work on Friday and tell you.

This always hurts my feelings because it makes me feel like he doesn't want to make plans with me, a loss of closeness, and it makes him feel like I'm trying to hem him in and limit him to a decision that he can't go back on.

Most of Tannen's claims about how differently men and women speak and how that can sometimes devastate a relationship can be founded not only on all of her examples, but in my life, too. I am relieved to know that what has caused me problems in my relationship with Chris is not an indication that the relationship is teetering on the trash basket, but is one that sometimes reflects the differences in gender and their speech. It is important to accept that there are gender differences, but that "the risk of ignoring these differences is greater than the danger of naming them. . . . Denying real differences can only compound the confusion that is already widespread in this era of shifting and re-forming relationships between women and men" (Tannen 16).

Instead of becoming dissatisfied with my relationship with Chris and getting frustrated when we try to talk things out, I am learning to take an approach that makes it possible to explain the dissatisfactions without blame and without throwing away the relationship. Understanding the differences between us and adjusting to them will chase the doubts and fears that haunt my sleep out of my mind, hopefully forever.

Here, the tenuousness of the connection between argument theory and real-life discourse shows up. Perhaps some would say that this paper isn't even an argument, since it is certainly a piece of self-expression.[5] But it seems clear to me that it is a substantiation argument, whose claim is that the writer's personal experiences with cross-sex discourse support Tannen's views (and that Tannen's views help the writer to understand and accept her experiences). But that is more complicated than just making a generalization from some examples.

Still, if we apply the STAR criteria sensitively, we can reveal some useful features of the text. The question of whether there is "sufficient" evidence is probably the trickiest one. There is certainly sufficient quotation from Tannen to establish her views on the topic of how men feel about consulting with the women in their lives about their plans. But Jonikka's major point is that Chris fits Tannen's portrait, and to show this we get only two instances of dialogue (plus a third that is presented as an atypical ideal). Perhaps the paper would be stronger with a third example (yet it is already over 1,100 words long). Both examples, however, reveal Chris's feelings of being "hemmed" in. In the first dialogue, he makes the point explicit: he doesn't like to feel as if he is reporting to his mother about when he is going where. Surely, we can take such a remark as a fairly significant *sign* of what he is going through. And the second example seems to be a repeated experience ("This always hurts my feelings").

    If the two examples are *typical* of Chris's behavior (rather than aberrations), then probably two from many, like one tablespoon from a cauldron of soup, are sufficient. And part of the point Jonikka, who should be something of an expert on the topic, is making is that they are "typical." She might of course be misperceiving matters on a topic of so much personal concern to her—but I think a reader is likely to be convinced, perhaps because Jonikka creates a strongly believable ethos. It's largely because of that ethos that a reader is willing to trust that the examples as reported are accurate and accurately interpreted (of course, the materials from Tannen can be checked). And surely anyone reading the two instances would say that they are relevant to the question of gender's role in language use and, specifically, to the accuracy of Tannen's claims about them. In my judgment, then, this is an effective argument for a variety of reasons, both rhetorical and logical.[6]

7 Arguing Evaluation Claims

The process of evaluation is, on the one hand, the most elusive and difficult of all reasoning activities and, on the other hand, the most important. It is the most important because it is the most closely tied to action.

—Michael Scriven (186)

The bottom line for me is persuasiveness. Evaluations, qualitative and quantitative, are forms of argument; one uses particular forms of argument— particular kinds of evidence, beliefs, warrants, reasons, propositions, and so on—to win the assent of particular audiences.

—Rexford Brown (115)

Humans evaluate continually: artwork, job applicants, student writing, automobiles, pizza, houses, universities, mass transit systems, athletes, restaurants, textbooks, circuses, the morality of abortion. You name it—somebody is evaluating it (or "assessing" it, to use our current educational jargon).

Stasis theory suggests that no matter what is being evaluated, a common matrix of issues must be discussed in order to establish a prima facie case for an evaluative claim. Whether we evaluate brands of lawn mowers or surrogate motherhood, the essential reasoning process is similar. It combines substantiation arguments with the strategy of argument by principle. (It may, of course, use any of the other GASCAP strategies as well.)

An old three-part heuristic defines the elements of a prima facie case for an evaluative argument. If one is trying to evaluate X, the formula says to ask,

1. What is the purpose of X?
2. How well does X fulfill its purpose?
3. Is the purpose worth fulfilling?

As an illustration, it's easy to see how that formula applies to evaluating consumer products. *Consumer Reports* uses it regularly when evaluating products ranging from disposable diapers to frozen dinners. The procedure is to agree upon the primary and important secondary purposes and from them to derive (usually by causal reasoning) some evaluation principles (or criteria or standards): together these principles serve as the argument warrant. Suppose the product is a tire. We know what a tire is supposed to do on a car, and from that knowledge, most of us can agree that a good tire must be durable, puncture resistant, easy and safe to handle, comfortable, and inexpensive. Such evaluative principles are causally related to the purpose: traits that help the item achieve its purpose are virtues, and traits that interfere with its achieving its purpose are weaknesses.

The warranting principles are partly context dependent. A good tire for a large automobile might not have the same traits that a good tire for a compact would have. And a good tire for lots of highway driving might differ from a good tire for in-town use. An evaluation can deal with this contextuality either by limiting the evaluation topic (such as "What is the best tire for my old car, to be used for short trips, given that expense is a major factor?") or by making several alternate contexts clear within the piece of writing (such as "For use on a second car to be driven for short distances at slow speeds, tire T is excellent, but for high-speed, long-distance driving, tire S is better").

Asserting that a standard is important is itself a matter for argument. My students almost uniformly maintain that a tire's appearance matters: they want to know whether it comes with raised white lettering and what the tread looks like, both of which strike me as irrelevant.

If the principles of evaluation are complex enough, whole pieces of discourse are devoted to arguing about a given standard. Such discourses (including questions like "What makes good poetry?" or "What are the qualities of an effective geometry teacher?") are called open-evaluation arguments. A discourse applying the standards to one or more specific instances is a closed evaluation.

So far I have stressed answering the first two questions in the heuristic, but the third one sometimes comes into play. Sometimes the item is only moderately successful, but the purpose is so crucial that even a moderate success is important (current medication used for assisting AIDS victims is a case in point). In other cases, the item undoubtedly fulfills its purpose, but doubt exists about whether the purpose is worth fulfilling. *Consumer Reports* once evaluated a new product, a receiver that brought in the audio portion of TV broadcasts. The product did indeed do what it said, with moderately good tone quality. But *Consumer Reports* doubted whether such a product served any need. The only people the writers could think of who might find it useful were blind consumers wanting to listen to TV shows, who could buy this receiver at less expense than a full TV set. I am reminded of those feats of incredible precision, like inscribing the Twenty-third Psalm on the head of a pin, or the sorts of achievements often memorialized in the *Guinness Book of World Records,* such as being able to spit a watermelon seed or throw a cow chip farther than any other living person. The best seed spitter in the world doesn't necessarily deserve much admiration.

There is also the problem of a product or action that achieves its purpose quite well, but over whose purpose there is evaluative contro-versy. The "abortion" pill, manufactured in France, achieves its pur-pose with a high degree of success. Does that make it a good product? What about an effective suicide machine? In terms of the Toulmin model, these issues shift the nexus of argument to backing for the warrant.

Evaluation in terms of purpose makes sense in a variety of con-texts: consumer products, teacher evaluation, evaluation of writing, aes-thetic evaluation, performance evaluation. But it is harder to apply such evaluation to moral and ethical questions. If we want to discuss the morality of abortion, evaluating it in terms of how well it achieves its purpose is largely beside the point since the real issue is whether its purpose is acceptable. Again, the argumentation shifts to the warrant itself and how it can be backed.

Still, underlying even moral evaluations is a framework similar to the one discussed above for products. You have to have criteria of evaluation to serve as warrants, but they come from different places and tend to be more problematic. One major argument leading to a nega-tive evaluation of abortion is based on our general value, the sanctity of life. Anti-abortionists often argue as follows:

> Abortion is the taking of a human life.
>
> Taking of human life is wrong.
>
> Therefore, abortion is wrong.

The opposition, however, counters that the premises are in error. Defenders of abortion point out that we regard the taking of human life as wrong only within limits: we do not believe human life is sacrosanct in the case of self-defense, or war, or in the case of a criminal convicted of a capital crime. Thus the universal warrant that *all* taking of human life is wrong can be disputed (in Toulmin terms, the anti-abortion argu-ment as given ignores important rebuttal conditions). And, of course, the defenders of abortion rights argue that aborting a fetus early in preg-nancy is not "taking" a human life, even though it is manifestly pre-venting a human life. Such a response has the effect of shifting the stasis, at least temporarily, to a question of definition as well as to an open-evaluation argument about the conditions under which it is acceptable to take a human life. Those who take the pro-choice position partly argue by analogy with other situations in which the taking of a human life is judged to be acceptable.

Fahnestock and Secor point out that the "subjects of evaluation are divided into four categories—things, people, acts, and finally abstractions" (*Rhetoric of Argument* 212). They then devote a useful section of their textbook to discussing the ways in which one applies the broad principles discussed here to evaluating things (natural, constructed, and aesthetic), people, actions, and abstractions like marriage or utilitarianism.

The requirements of the prima facie case for an evaluation, then, include a set of criteria, support for any criteria that might be challenged, plus data about the case at hand and how the data fit the criteria. Such arguments commonly fall into one of three similar structures. The first is the *Consumer Reports* structure, in which the standards of evaluation to be used are announced initially and defended in one section and then are applied in a second one. Following this structure involves, first, writing an open-evaluation essay and, second, using it to write a closed one. The structure has the virtues of clarity and thoroughness since it forces writers to be explicit about their standards of judgment, something most of us are all too willing to ignore when we make assertions like "His behavior was completely unethical" or "That was an awful movie."

But this structure also highlights one major difficulty with all evaluation. Suppose one has three criteria for judging teachers and thus wants to make use of the following argument form:

WARRANT: All good teachers have traits A, B, and C.

DATA: Professor DeBrain has traits A, B, and C.

CLAIM: Professor DeBrain is a good teacher.

Examining the planned reasoning, the writer should notice a problem with the argument: unless traits A, B, and C are *sufficient* to guarantee effective teaching, the conclusion doesn't follow. As stated, the warrant says that the three traits are *necessary* for a good teacher, not that they are *sufficient*. (Technically, the argument is a syllogism with an undistributed middle term. See Appendix B.) The student might then recast the argument as follows:

WARRANT: All teachers with traits A, B, and C are good teachers.

DATA: Professor DeBrain has traits A, B, and C.
CLAIM: Professor DeBrain is a good teacher.

All right. Now the conclusion would follow from the premises. But the warrant is going to be hard to prove. It's harder to show that *any* teacher with these traits will be a good teacher no matter what other factors are present than merely to show that all good teachers share these traits (which is difficult enough). And then suppose that the evidence for the minor premise shows that DeBrain actually lacks trait A but has traits B and C. She doesn't, therefore, quite fit within the category the warrant deals with, but she's close.

At this point the writer has to decide whether all the traits are necessary or whether they are somehow additive, so that having most of them makes someone a good teacher even though others are lacking. And if they are additive, are some more important than others, so that lacking certain ones is merely a minor weakness? The procedure isn't very different from trying to evaluate student essays. We have a whole set of criteria in mind that are relevant to a paper's being good, but some are necessary and some are useful extras. Some are necessary for some papers and some for all. And the final evaluation isn't just the binary of yes/good—no/bad, but a variable measure in which some good ones are better than other good ones. This means that in articulating the standards in the first place, we must consider their relative importance.

All of these problems exist no matter which structure an evaluative argument uses. This first form merely illustrates them most clearly.

A second structure is very similar, but the evaluative principles are distributed throughout the text, which works back and forth between a standard and its application. A standard is announced, explained, defended, and then applied before the argument goes to the second one. The structure is just as explicit as the previous one but arranges the material differently.

Finally, one can argue enthymematically by using a series of claims about the entity being evaluated without making the standards explicit. In my experience, this is the most common structure. It works well when the evaluation is for an audience familiar with the general issues, such as in a review of a new mystery novel written for fans of the genre. On the other hand, such a structure often hides significant issues relevant to an evaluation because it avoids arguing the open-evaluation issues upon which the application is necessarily based. A writer using this structure assumes that the criteria need no clarification or defense, even in regard to their relative weight. If the audience is willing to make such an assumption, there is no problem. But if the audience challenges any of the assumptions, then the writer has lost the opportunity to support part of the argument.

Let's look at some examples of student writing that use this sort of structure. Diana Martin, a first-year honors student, was seriously involved in preparing for a synchronized swimming show during the semester in which the first piece was written. Her English professor made the mistake one day of alluding negatively to all the time she was expending on the show. This was her journal entry for the next class period, complete with title:

Tread Lightly as You Walk on the Water

At the beginning of Friday morning's English class, it was suggested to me that perhaps I should become involved in an activity a bit more complicated and worthwhile than the ETSU Water Show. Just to set matters straight, I can see nothing else at this time that is any more complicated or worthwhile than the water show. Water ballet stunts, although many may appear simple to the untrained eye, are in fact very strenuous and difficult to do. Next time you go swimming try floating on your back while one leg is extended straight at a 90 degree angle to the rest of your body. Hard to do? Don't be funny—that's one of the most basic stunts of water ballet. Here's another to try since that one was so easy, it's called a "catalina." All you have to do is float on your back, extend one leg straight at a 90 degree angle to the rest of your body, twist your body without moving the extended leg, and dive straight downward, having both feet meet as they enter the water. Now that you have mastered these two stunts with such ease, try them in synchrony with another swimmer.

Now, as far as the show not being a very worthwhile activity, think again! To me the show is extremely worthwhile for several reasons. Basically, constant and vigorous work-outs keep me physically fit which is an asset to my health. The show also gives me an outlet for pent-up energy and helps me to relax. The progress that I have made from last semester's show to now has boosted my self-confidence. And my hours of practice have been rewarded by my becoming one of the principals for the upcoming show. That in itself makes every bit of effort that I put into the show worthwhile. And, since I plan to minor in therapeutic recreation, the show is a learning experience, especially since the coach is a therapeutic recreation doctoral student. You still may not see the water show as worthwhile, but you can't say it's hurting me, after all, I managed a 3.83 GPA with 17 hours last semester!

Considering that we are studying inductive reasoning in class, I would like to hear some examples of why you don't think the show is complicated or worthwhile enough. How many Water Shows have you seen on which you can base your conclusion? Tread lightly as you walk on the water—I may be underneath the water and grab you by the leg and pull you under.

How would you like it if I suggested you find something more worth-while than tennis?

This is a pretty good illustration of an evaluation argument constructed enthymematically. Diana defends her participation in water ballet against two alleged attacks on its value: (1) that the activity isn't demanding enough and (2) that it takes up too much time for its value. Her first paragraph shows with details that water ballet is difficult, with an unstated premise, apparently accepted by both the writer and, in the writer's view, the teacher who made the earlier criticism—that "an activity that isn't demanding isn't valuable." For the record, I don't believe I said it wasn't demanding enough. But I may have said something about its not being intellectually challenging. There is actually a logical problem here, since an activity can be extremely demanding yet be of little value. Still, as a refutation of the charge Diana understood to have been made, the argument is effective.

In her second paragraph, Diana defends the intrinsic worth of water ballet for her. Her first defense is that practicing for the ballet is good exercise that keeps her fit and healthy. The unstated value premise that staying fit and healthy is good scarcely needs any defense. She similarly defends the activity on the grounds of boosting self-confidence (also an obvious value in our culture). Finally, since her major field is recreational therapy, and since her coach is a recreational therapist, she learns something from the activity that will be valuable to her professional future. This argument, when examined, is a bit more vague, since it is unlikely that water ballet would actually be used as therapy for anyone. Finally, Diana turns to a more direct answer to her opponent, an answer some would characterize as a fallacious *ad hominem* (see Chapter 9). She says both that the critic should quit acting as if he believes he can make godlike judgments and that his own participation in tennis makes him ill-qualified to criticize someone else's recreational choices. In my view, the wit and playful tone of the conclusion make it effective and move it out of the realm of systematic argument, so any charge of fallacy is wrongheaded.

Diana's piece was a journal arising out of the real rhetorical context of the classroom. When I assign an evaluation essay, however, I often ask students to evaluate a particular teacher they have had. The assignment has the virtue of working at a variety of educational levels, of being about issues students have specific knowledge of, and of being easily adapted to some real rhetorical situation. I suggest that students may write the paper as a letter to the teacher (in which case I ask them to send it). Or they might make it a letter to an administrator or the school board. Or it could be written for other students who might take the teacher, or for students who are thinking of becoming teachers. Sandy McCray, a freshman, chose to write to the student body of her high school:

Take Perault . . . Please!

My sophomore year in high school was filled with advice from upperclassmen on items such as what classes to take and what teachers to get or to avoid. I half-listened to most of what they had to say and then put it out of my mind. Most of it, that is, except for one tidbit that was given to me by more people than not: "Take Perault's class! It's great!" I'm not one to make judgments based only on hearsay, so I decided to take his Civil Liberties class and see what made it so popular. What I found was not only awe-inspiring material but also a fantastic teacher, the best that I had in my entire four years of high school.

Mr. Perault was a well-built, hairy-chested, blond-haired, blue-eyed dream come true as far as looks were concerned. I never heard any complaints about having to watch him while he lectured, especially when he got back from a Spring Vacation he spent in the Bahamas. His cocoa brown tan contrasted so beautifully with his white smile and yellow terry cloth shirt!! Yet, his looks seem somewhat insignificant when you see the terrific class he ran.

Before the start of each class period, there were notes for that day's lecture written on the blackboard. They were in outline form for the student's convenience in copying them down. Mr. Perault always said he would rather that we could concentrate more on what he was saying than trying to write down everything he said. He would lecture over the notes from the board, going into more specifics than that basic outline. But that basic outline would keep him and the student on track of what he had and hadn't covered, so each class (he taught six periods of this subject) got basically the same lecture. That way, when we had a test, there was no chance of being asked a question that he hadn't covered in every class he taught.

Not only were Mr. Perault's lectures easy to follow, they held very vivid examples of points he was trying to make. One time he was telling us about the hardships that blacks faced as they began their fight for acceptance into white colleges. He told us how some of the teachers in these colleges would go as far as to make black students sit in the hall to listen to lectures; how they were isolated from the group. To demonstrate how awkward this would be in a learning situation, Mr. Perault lectured to us for about fifteen minutes from out in the hall. Believe me, we got the point!

Another day he was lecturing on the different kinds of evidence that may be used in a court of law. One of the other Social Studies teachers, Mr. Dickinson, burst in the room and began yelling at Mr. Perault about a stack of ungraded papers. The two argued back and forth for a few minutes when, suddenly, Mr. Dickinson pulled out a gun, shot Mr. Perault, and dashed out of the room! As Mr. Perault fell to the floor, he told everyone to get out a piece of paper and, without looking around, write everything they saw: what each of the men had been wearing, what they were arguing about, etc. It had been a cap gun, of course, and Mr. Perault collected our papers when we were finished. He then proceeded to read each eyewitness account of the incident. Every paper sounded so different from the one before it that you would not have thought we had seen the same occurrence. He proved to us that eyewitness accounts are not always the solid, unquestionable evidence that many people believe them to be.

Yes, Mr. Perault made everything very clear, yet he made it enjoyable too. It is because of this that I dare to say that his students retained their knowledge not just until after a test was over, but for many years to come. From my senior year on I have been giving sophomores at Green Mountain High School the same advice that I got, "Take Perault's class! It's great!"

Now, certainly, a serious critic can easily find features of this essay to criticize, such as the apparent assumption that good teachers lecture to students and the paragraph about Perault's appearance. Perhaps more important, one could ask about omissions: what sorts of tests and projects were given, how was the course graded, what about student participation and critical thinking? But for my money, this is strong evaluative writing, given that the author is a first-year college student and that the intended audience is students in high school. Judging by its structure, however, I would have to work to pull out exactly what "criteria" were being used to make the evaluation.

Another common evaluative writing project in English classes is the evaluative paper about a text read for class, whether it is framed as a book review or as a judgment growing out of issues raised by the in-class reading. Here is a negative evaluation that grew out of class discussion of Deborah Tannen's *You Just Don't Understand:*

Warning to Males
by Duane Fields

This is a caution to males that plan to read the book *You Just Don't Understand: Women and Men in Conversation* by Deborah Tannen. The "You" stands for males. But because of Tannen's apparent bias toward women, men who read this book hoping to learn how conversation of both males and females could improve will be disturbed by the many examples that, even prefaced with a disclaimer, imply the men to be the source of the problem and make them look bad.

I would like to point out, that Tannen discusses men and women in general and does not fault all of one gender. Throughout these several statements Tannen tries to instill in the reader that she is not blaming all men or all women for the problems that exist in conversation between the genders. Even so, many examples do not seem to follow her prefaces.

At the beginning of the book there is a section titled "The Modern Face of Chivalry" (34–35). In this section Tannen discusses that men yield the right of way or hold a door open to establish status and connection. The status by taking control and the connection by being nice. In her example the man yielding the right of way in traffic is causing the woman to be a subordinate. In my interpretation of these circumstances, it is for the sole reason of politeness that the man offers the right of way to the woman. Tannen says that a man probably only thinks of the polite interpretation of the action. Tannen is suggesting that involuntarily men are seeking control of women and other men in their actions of politeness. Thus by being polite men are really trying to control those around them.

In the section "I'll Fix It For You" Tannen frames men as "problem solvers." This is not what women want, nor is it what should be done according to Tannen. Tannen says that problems should be equaled not solved. When men attempt to solve problems they are sending the metamessage, the underlying meaning of a statement, that "We're not the same. You have the problems; I have the solutions" (53). In this section, once again, the men look bad in the example.

The last paragraph of "Mutual Accusations" (143) shows women suffering in conversation because of men. Tannen says "that it is true . . . that men listen to women less frequently than women listen to men." She goes on to say that men do not want to listen for a long time because it frames them as subordinate. Women like to listen. This makes men sound uncaring and indifferent. If men felt that listening made them a subordinate then why would they listen at all? The answer is that men do not listen less frequently than women and the length does not matter. Tannen has failed again in her attempt not to be biased.

The section of "Hope for the Future" (148) gives the impression that women should change their approach to conversation because men can't. The whole section is devoted to women inserting themselves into conversation. That sounds good except that the last paragraph deals with men. Tannen says that men would find conversation easier if they would just listen. This statement makes men sound bad again. Tannen implies through this statement that all men do is talk and find it hard to listen to women. Tannen ends the section with an anecdote of a woman who is looking for a man that asks how her day was and really wants to know. To place this at the end, emphasizes to the reader the bad aspect of men's listening that Tannen is trying to get across.

In chapter seven men were used in a positive way in some of the examples. But the very last section, "Who's Driving?" (215) ends the chapter making men look bad. Tannen suggests men find a conversation to be a contest that does not support the other's talk. The way in which she states this makes it sound as if she is not insisting all men do this. But she goes on to counter this statement with one that backs up women's feeling that they are being violated in the "game" of conversation. Thus making the women look good as the sufferers of men's competition. Further, she comes close to defending men in the fact that she says women's insistence of support can be annoying. That was the first part of the sentence. The rest says that men view conversation as a fight ("verbal sparring"). "And a left jab . . . can become a knockout if your opponent's [a woman's] fists are not raised to fight." This is a slam to men. This idea infers that men are always looking for a fight in a conversation and do not care about women's feelings.

These interpretations of Tannen may not be popular with female fans of this book, but males need to know about the possibility of finding these derogatory inferences. Throughout the book it is the women who are pictured as suffering in conversation because of men. This warning is not to deter men from reading *You Just Don't Understand* because there are some good things to be found in this book, but be prepared males.

Throughout our two-week discussion of Tannen's book, Duane (and other members of the class) had accused Tannen of what they termed "male bashing." In this final evaluation essay, written for supposed publication as a column in our campus newspaper, Duane addresses male students who have not read the book, attempting to support the claim that Tannen is biased against males by providing a considerable list of examples. At several points, Duane tries valiantly, but largely unsuccessfully, I think, to acknowledge an opposing view by pointing out that Tannen frequently says she is blaming neither sex for the frequent failures to communicate, but simply saying that they speak different genderlects, which are often misunderstood by the other. I'm not sure the examples as presented would make sense to students who had not yet read the book, and certainly, even the examples given can be read in other ways. Some of them seem to me to be taken out of Tannen's context and misinterpreted, and as some of my graduate students pointed out, Duane never lets Tannen speak for herself in direct quotation. Further, it isn't clear whether Duane is saying that it's a bad book (which might be rhetorically awkward in a paper that must be evaluated by a teacher who had selected the book and spoken favorably of it in class) or just that it has one defect. Even though he acknowledges that the book has "some good things," certainly the thrust of the argument is to make a negative judgment, since in a book claiming to treat male and female language use fairly, being biased against the gendered usage of one sex would surely be a major defect. Still, I was impressed with Duane's courage in making the argument and with the fairly elaborate development included in the paper. Yet, finally, I am ambivalent about the paper. It could be so much better done than it is. And when I have used the paper with workshops of graduate assistants practicing how to evaluate and write useful comments to students, reactions to the paper have ranged all across the board, but few of the assistants who saw it as a poor paper were able to be very precise about its weaknesses.

Probably the most difficult sort of evaluation, one which students are simultaneously willing to say cannot be argued yet willing to assert claims about, is moral evaluation of an act. (Acts can also be evaluated aesthetically, pragmatically on the basis of outcome, even competitively in terms of skill levels.) It's important that we disabuse students of the equally extreme views that moral value judgments are "just matters of opinion" and thus cannot be argued at all and that value judgments are simple and obvious claims on which all right-thinking people agree. Value judgments are in the realm of the contingent. They are questions of "ought," not "is," to use a distinction common in philosophy. But they are not purely relative matters of personal taste either. People can and must argue thoughtfully about them.[7]

In an interesting and readable book, *The Moral Imperative*, Vincent Ryan Ruggiero has presented a useful first-order discussion of how we go about making moral judgments. He teaches students that in order to evaluate the morality of an act, one asks three questions:

1. What are the likely consequences of the act?
2. What accepted ideals does the act comply with or contradict?
3. What commitments on the part of the actor does the act meet or violate? (see 55–57)

Ruggiero says that we evaluate all acts on the basis of some combination of these considerations. The first one, asking about the outcomes of the act, is pragmatic. The second allows us to consider a variety of widely acceptable moral precepts such as "respect for human life." And the third considers promises made by the actor. Most complex acts, when subjected to these three questions, lead to a variety of inconsistent evaluative claims, and the questions themselves hide considerable complexity. (Judging the outcomes as good or bad is problematic; even predicting those outcomes often requires difficult causal reasoning. And deciding what moral precepts are widely acceptable is certainly tough.)

To challenge my students in learning how to think through such matters, I often present them with modern moral dilemmas, some of them made up, some taken from real situations. One illustration involves the case of David and Ginger Twitchell, whose $2\frac{1}{2}$-year-old son, Robyn, died of a bowel obstruction. The Twitchells are Christian Scientists, and as such, they did not seek medical help for Robyn but did call on the services of a "practitioner" from their church to pray for the child. Robyn died in April of 1986, and the Twitchells were tried in Boston in 1990. The trial lasted two months, and the Twitchells were found guilty of involuntary manslaughter and sentenced to ten years' probation and the requirement that their two other children be evaluated regularly by a physician (see Starr; Sanders).

The case thus pits two fundamental values against each other—freedom to practice one's religion against the rights of children not to be abused. Most of my students come from traditional protestant religious backgrounds, but almost unanimously they agree that the Twitchells are guilty. And, initially, it doesn't seem like a complex issue to them: parents must take good care of their children, and calling in a religious practitioner to pray over a deadly condition that surgery could easily solve doesn't satisfy them, especially when they are told that during his testimony, Mr. Twitchell said that should the same situation occur in the future to one of his other two children, he would act in the same way. But in-class discussion about the implications of such a position soon makes their lives complicated. They are obviously judging primarily by "consequences" in Ruggiero's scheme and not taking ideals, even their own, into account. Some of them want simply to argue that Christian Science is wrong about rejecting the use of medical treatments, and that leads us to discussing whether the state has the right to impose biblical readings on a religion (invariably, other religious views, from Mormonism to snake handling and peyote use, come up in the discussion as potentially relevant analogies). And my students are shocked when they learn that the Massachusetts statute on child abuse and neglect creates an explicit exemption for those who believe in spiritual healing (as do the laws in nearly all states).

Others argue that it's just foolish to rely on prayer when medical science would do the job. But that tends to call into question the seriousness of their own religious beliefs, since most of them do believe in praying to an omniscient God. Some point out that we would not have medical care if it were not part of God's plan, but then they realize that forcing the Twitchells to accept that view doesn't protect the freedom to practice a widely held religious viewpoint, a freedom seemingly guaranteed by the Massachusetts law. And we go round and round in class discussions. (For the record, the Twitchells' conviction was overturned by the Massachusetts Supreme Court in 1993. See "Christian Scientists Are Cleared of Manslaughter.")

So as with other argumentative stases, the writer faces the problem of weighing a variety of arguments pro and con. Ruggiero does not say that taking this approach will resolve moral issues. But he does assert that taking it will lead to a more thorough and thoughtful analysis of the moral judgment, whatever it is. We can hardly expect student writers to solve problems that have perplexed moral philosophers through the ages. We *can* expect students to learn more about the complexities of the questions. They may still fail to reach a "correct" answer, but to borrow a phrase from Jim Corder of Texas Christian University, they will "fail at a higher level."

8 Arguing Policy Claims

In the sequential hierarchy of argumentative claims, policy argumentation, argumentation over what should or should not be done, is the most complex. Unfortunately, many English teachers automatically equate "argument" with policy argument. Sometimes they join this view with the idea that students should be learning to write about public issues in a democracy, so they assign capital punishment or abortion or assisted suicide or a state lottery as policy topics. If tasks like this are ever assigned—and about these I have real doubts—they should come only after students have been taught the features needed to create a prima facie policy argument and have tried their hand at policy arguments closer to their own lives.

In Texas each year, every high school freshman must write a policy argument as part of a battery of achievement tests. One year, for example, freshmen were asked to write a letter to their principal arguing whether or not a wooded portion of the school grounds should be used to construct a new parking lot.

That assignment is better than many policy assignments since it (1) provides an audience to be addressed and (2) involves a limited topic that the students would have at least some knowledge of and interest in. But Texas high school freshmen are unlikely to have been taught anything about what is needed in a good policy essay. Nor would many students actually have the relevant information needed to deal with that question, such as how many students and staff drive cars to school, how much parking space is now available, what would it cost to build the lot, and whether the lot could be built in other places. Fortunately for the students, these tests are scored holistically and at a fairly basic level: if a paper is on-topic, coherent (takes a position and gives several reasons for it), and reasonably free from sentence-level and mechanical problems, it passes.

In one sense, policy argument is a special case of evaluative writing. We have a series of options (alternative policies) to be assessed vis-à-vis each other: to use the test prompt as an example, the options include leaving things as they are, building a new parking lot (in several possible locations), or restricting the number of cars allowed. With those given, the writer must decide the relevant criteria for evaluation and then make a comparative analysis of which one is best.

But policy argument is so common at all levels of society that ever since the Greek rhetoricians identified deliberative rhetoric as a major type, a model of how policy argumentation works has been emerging. It simply codifies what some of the major criteria for evaluating proposed policies ought to be, recognizing that all three of Ruggiero's dimensions of moral evaluation are relevant, but that in practical terms, the outcomes of policies receive the most attention.

We face policy arguments everywhere. They are the bulk of all committee work; they are what all legislative bodies—from faculty senates, to city commissions, to federal and state legislatures—deal with regularly. They are also a constant concern within the family: "What time should the children go to bed?" "Should we buy a new car?" "Should we accept the new job offer and move?" "Should we eat out tonight?" "Should we have a party?" "Should we have children?" Somebody said, "The trouble with life is, it's just one damn thing after another," and those things generally involve policy decisions.

Policy arguments come in all sizes. They run from "Should I wash these jeans in hot or cold water?" to the national issues of health insurance, the budget deficit, gun control, and affirmative action. Whether one deliberates over buying ground chuck, hamburger, or neither, or over supporting a prayer-in-the-schools amendment, stasis theory says that all of them are argued in similar ways, ways that one can learn and apply, no matter what the issue. Over the years they have been codified into the *stock issues* of policy argumentation.

Composition texts and logic books rarely treat these concerns (analyses of recommendation reports in some books on technical writing are one exception). But they are discussed regularly and at length in speech textbooks, especially those focused on competitive debate. Presentations of these issues vary somewhat, but the four standard ones are

- Need
- Plan
- Advantages of Plan
- Disadvantages of Plan

Any policy argument that does not somehow address all of these is incomplete, although, occasionally, only one side may be presented, on the assumption that in the entire rhetorical context, someone else will present arguments for the other side. It is permissible to write an essay limited to "The Case for Metal Detectors in Our School," as long as the writer does not claim this is the same as showing that metal detectors should be installed.

Since we normally engage in policy argument when we perceive a problem or inadequacy in our current way of doing things, the first point to be shown (this is logical priority; it need not be presented first in the discourse) is that something is wrong now. A new policy should be adopted if the present policy leads to problems, evils, harms, weaknesses—and if a new policy can be found that remedies them. As the old Texas adage has it, "If'n it ain't broke, don't fix it."

Substantiating the existence of such conditions and evaluating that they are indeed problems establish a *need* for a change. To handle this stock issue, the arguer must be sure to understand what the present system is and who is harmed by it. A recent example springs to mind of a student who proposed a major overhaul of the junior-level essay at my university. His major argument was that the current test was administered unfairly and to the disadvantage of students since the English department evaluated it. He argued that not only do English teachers apply unique and unrealistic standards to writing, but that they also have a vested interest in failing students in order to generate enrollment in a special advanced-level remedial course. The student was unaware that the English department plays no role in evaluating the junior-level essay. Often, students working on such local policy arguments need to be encouraged to interview those who work with the policy. That has the dual advantage of allowing them to become familiar with the policy and also of learning why it was enacted. One of my students once wanted to argue for more vegetarian main dishes in our school cafeteria, but he gave it up as untenable after interviewing the local head of our food service.

One conventional way to present a need argument is to first give it a name, such as "The present law causes *severe economic hardship for families of alcoholics.*" Then, the nature of the problems must be *explained.* This involves defining what is meant by "severe economic hardship" and showing *causally* how the current system creates the hardship. Then, a substantiation argument must be used to show that the conditions asserted actually exist and exist widely enough to cause concern. This can involve all of the usual GASCAP modes of substantiation. Here, the writer must create in the audience more than a logical perception of the problem but also an emotional commitment to solving it. To use Perelman and Olbrechts-Tyteca's term, the arguer must give the problem *presence* for the audience (115–20). Or to use classical rhetoric's term, the arguer must use *pathos.*

Once a need has been established, or agreed to without argument, the arguer outlines exactly what must be done to meet the need (solve the problem, remove the evil). In essence, the arguer must engage in a cost/benefits analysis of the plan, but "cost/benefits" must be understood as a metaphor for all the consequences of the proposal, both valued and problematic. The central warrant for all policy argument:

> If a plan is to be adopted at all, its advantages must outweigh its disadvantages.

Frequently, several possible solutions suggest themselves, and the arguer must discuss each to see how well it meets the problem and what new problems it creates. Some years ago, Commerce, Texas, faced a major water shortage. There was no disagreement over the existence of the problem: clearly, the artesian wells that supplied the city were running dry. So our policy concerns did not focus on the need, which was acknowledged. We stressed instead the relative merits of several different proposals: (1) a relatively cheap proposal involved running a pipeline to a nearby town and buying treated water from them, and (2) a somewhat more expensive suggestion involved tapping into this town's water supply at a spot prior to their treatment plant. That would mean building our own treatment facilities, but the cost per gallon of untreated water would be less than the cost of already-treated water. (3) Finally, there was the BMW. We could build our own pipeline, a longer one, to the same lake the neighboring city used, build our own pumping station and our own treatment facility. This was a much more expensive plan, but one which would not leave us dependent on the future decisions of another corporate entity. In a rare show of willingness to raise taxes for the public weal, we chose the third option because most voters were convinced it was the wisest in the long run, despite its cost.

We based our reasoning on this corollary of the central warrant:

> If one plan is to be adopted over others, the cost/benefit ratio must be higher for the adopted plan than for any others proposed.

These principles imply that a full policy argument should always take into account the potential disadvantages of one's proposal. They should be acknowledged, minimized wherever possible, refuted when false, and admitted, but counterbalanced by the advantages, when appropriate. No plan is perfect. Every plan will have some undesirable consequences for someone. The wise, not to mention fair, arguer will not ignore these outcomes but will deal with them. And if, after serious thought, the arguer cannot find a way to alleviate serious negative consequences, then he or she should consider reversing the claim being argued. Changing one's mind during writing is no sin.

In introductory speech courses some years ago, students commonly had to give what was called a "problem/solution" speech. They were to locate a social problem, present it to the audience with adequate data to be convincing, and suggest a solution—usually in ten minutes. What often happened was that the student spent eight and a half minutes on the problem and then proposed briefly one or two steps that might be taken to deal with it, usually including the American panacea, "We need to educate the public about. . . ."

Such discourse fails as policy argument, for no time is spent discussing how the "solution" would actually solve the problem presented, and no time is spent considering the solution's disadvantages. On the other hand, sometimes the closing policy recommendation could be considered a mere rhetorical peroration meant not to settle what should be done but to provoke further discourse. In that case, the argument was actually substantiation and evaluation rather than recommendation. That is a perfectly legitimate type of discourse, yet it leaves someone else to engage in the dirty work of solving the problem thus identified. (But then, often, that's what we have committees and legislative bodies for.)

There are at least as many different ways to organize a policy argument as there are policies to be argued. George Orwell's essay "A Hanging" is, finally, a policy argument against capital punishment, but it is written entirely as a personal narrative of the events one morning in India when, before breakfast, Orwell had to participate in hanging a prisoner. Utopian novels are large-scale policy arguments, as are many social protest plays and novels. Satire is frequently an artistic mode of policy argument.

But given the importance of the four stock issues, several traditional structures exist for making policy arguments. And it might be helpfully liberating if our students became aware of these possibilities. One procedure simply follows the stock issues themselves. After an introduction, the problems of the present system are demonstrated and analyzed causally, a plan is proposed (or perhaps several of them), the obvious disadvantages of the proposed plan(s) are discussed and minimized (assuming one is arguing for a change; if not, the disadvantages are stressed), and the advantages of the new plan vis-à-vis the current system are demonstrated. Often, it is in this step, showing that the plan would actually alleviate the problems demonstrated, that student policy writing is weakest. It requires causal speculation about future events, which is difficult. And it means going back to the specific evidence used to show the problem and indicating, step by step, how the instances of the problem would not have occurred if the new plan had been in effect instead of the old one.

The alternate, but also standard, structure is to begin with the plan. It is announced early as a thesis. Again, its disadvantages are considered and minimized. But then the arguer writes the bulk of the paper on the advantages of the proposal. And each advantage is developed in the comparison-contrast mode, showing simultaneously the virtues of the new proposal and the weaknesses of the current system. The need issue, thus, is not ignored; it's just moved.

If a writer wants to use this second scheme but is arguing against changing from the current way of doing things, the potential advantages of the proposal are discussed and minimized first; then, the ways in which the proposal would cause new problems (disadvantages) are stressed.

To illustrate how stasis theory, and argumentation theory in general, show up in real discourse, recall the *Newsweek* column by Kandy Stroud about pornographic rock lyrics, introduced in Chapter 3. Stroud's essay first attempts to argue a substantiation claim, primarily by generalization. The claim is summed up in the phrases "increasingly explicit nature of rock music" and "Unabashedly sexual lyrics like these, augmented by orgasmic moans and howls, compose the musical diet millions of children are now being fed at concerts, on albums, on radio and MTV." The generalization rests on seven examples of rock lyrics.

If we evaluate the argument using the STAR system, and taking into account the context that *Newsweek* "My Turn" columns are limited to 1,100 words, we would, I think, conclude that

1. seven examples is probably sufficient to demonstrate the existence of the explicit lyrics to *Newsweek* readers;

2. the examples are probably *not* typical since Stroud has chosen the most extreme ones as a basis for her later value argument (but this does not injure the argument);

3. the examples are probably accurate (*Newsweek*'s reputation is part of the grounds for such a decision, and readers can check much of the material for themselves; moreover, the examples are detailed and specific enough to sound credible); and

4. the examples certainly are relevant to the conclusion because any reader will agree that they are sexually explicit.

Since part of Stroud's substantiation argument is not just that rock lyrics are sexually explicit but that they are becoming more so, she compares sexual lyrics of 1985 songs against those of her own youth, concluding that "innuendo has given way to the overt." Most of her readers will probably accept on the grounds of their own experience that rock music lyrics twenty years earlier, while sexual, were not explicitly so like the ones she has cited, so this argument seems soundly developed, given the rhetorical context.

Stroud's further argument that these sexually explicit lyrics are a problem is naturally of a different sort. Essentially, she argues from the effect of the explicit lyrics, claiming that music can degrade and presumably intending her readers to understand that sexually explicit music is degrading in ways that the sexually implicit rock of her youth was not.

Granted, cause and effect is a standard basis for an evaluative argument, but demonstrating that the causal chain actually exists requires a second substantiation argument. And here Stroud's case weakens considerably. She cites the facts that some drug programs forbid teenagers to go to rock concerts and that some schools which prohibit smoking and drinking also prohibit rock music. Apparently these are enthymematic arguments, which, if expanded, are meant to look like this:

> Things banned by these schools and groups are [probably] harmful.
>
> Rock music is banned by these schools and groups.
>
> Therefore rock music is [probably] harmful.

This is a valid argument structure with a warrant, grounds, an adverbial qualifier, and a claim, but there is considerable doubt that the warrant is true. So, it is at best a weak argument, at least for a national and disparate audience.

Stroud also argues the value case by authority. Aristotle is quoted, but only for a general notion, since he did not say anything about sexually explicit rock music. One major "authority" is Dr. Novello, whom Stroud qualifies only as being director of a drug program (perhaps the same one referred to earlier), but he doesn't say the explicit lyrics have harmful effects. What he says is that he asks the teenagers brought to him what sort of music they listen to because it tells him something about them. He mentions only three kinds of music, as if there were no others, but presumably he has also learned that if a child listens to country and western music or to Bach, such behavior would also help him understand the child's state of mind. In other words, the authority's testimony here does not seem directly relevant to the claim being argued. (Conceivably, however, Stroud knows more of the context of the quotation, which might make it relevant.)

The other major "authority" is Father James Connor, who says that "rock is turning sex into something casual . . . as if society is encouraging its youngsters to get sexually involved." Whether Father Connor is an expert on either rock music or its effects is certainly questionable, but on the other hand, even Stroud's reader can tell from the lyrics quoted that in some rock songs, sex—even violent sex—is treated in a manner that might well be called casual. Whether songs like those quoted encourage youth to get involved in sexual activities is a questionable causal assertion, but one could interpret the argument as resting on the unexpressed warrant that whatever is treated casually is more likely to be engaged in than something that is treated more circumspectly. Whether being "sexually involved" is wrong is not argued. Presumably, a Catholic priest would take that as a given, and since Stroud several times refers to the audience of these lyrics as "children," the argument may also rest on the no doubt widely shared assumption that "children should not be sexually involved."

Probably, the major evaluation argument is the submerged one that relies partly on the reader's sense of shock after reading the lyrics, a sense of shock that the reader probably shares with Stroud. We don't want our "children" exposed to such gross images as public masturbation, oral sex forced at gunpoint, and violent bloody rape via buzz saw. In paragraph two, Stroud refers to these lyrics as a "musical diet," and the metaphor is picked up in the final paragraph with a call for a "healthy" diet of music that is good for the consumer. There is a traditional argument by analogy submerged in that metaphor. Eating nutritious food builds strong bodies, but eating corrupt food corrupts the body.

Stroud's argument is weakest when she moves to the stasis of recommendation. The recommendations get only two of eleven paragraphs, and the whole discourse reminds me of the problem-solution speeches I described earlier. Actually, three possible solutions are mentioned: parental control of what children listen to, "legislative action," and "a measure of self-restraint." She doesn't seem to take the first two seriously, but she does make a pair of arguments for self-restraint from the industry or the rock stars themselves. She compares the rock music industry to the liquor industry and argues by analogy that if liquor advertising can be voluntarily kept off the public airwaves, then the record industry ought to be able to curb porn rock. But the analogy is faulty in that it compares voluntarily limiting advertising for a product (liquor) to limiting a product itself (rock music): the one does not come over the air; thus the other could also be removed. But rock music isn't part of *advertising* on the air; it is part of the programming. To ask the music industry to restrict itself is like asking the liquor industry to voluntarily cut out all liquors over a certain proof.

Then, Stroud compares the efforts of rock musicians to donate their services for African famine relief to the possibility of their doing similar charitable work by not making sexually explicit songs. That analogy also breaks down badly. In the first place, presumably the rock groups do not agree that their songs are harmful; thus they have no motive for voluntary action. In the second place, raising money for charity took the cooperation of only a segment of the industry, but to prevent the lyrics Stroud objects to would take unanimity of action. If fifteen major rock stars did not appear for African relief, that would not be a major problem in raising money, but if as many as five or ten stars made successful, sexually explicit songs, the pornography Stroud objects to would not be stopped.

Finally, I suggested that refutation ought to be a part of any argument, and Stroud seems not to acknowledge that there may well be people who would not see these sexually explicit lyrics as a problem. Her opponents might point out that these lyrics are not widespread enough to have a serious impact, that they are defensible on the grounds of free speech, that the authorities she cites would be equally critical of the implicit sexuality of the rock lyrics she does not oppose, and that her proposed solutions would not work and would lead to new problems.

As a substantiation argument calling the attention of readers to a phenomenon that they were perhaps not aware of and ought to be, Stroud's essay seems, to me, effective. As a value argument, it is weaker but still makes a possible case. As a policy recommendation, it is unsatisfactory.

Teaching students the major elements of a prima facie case for a policy argument, as well as some of the standard structures used, can be very valuable. They can use the elements as heuristics when planning an argument, as revision criteria when rewriting, and as critical-thinking probes whenever they are confronted with a policy argument from someone else, as I have just done with Stroud's essay.

I regularly assign a policy essay toward the end of a first-year college composition course that has been built largely around the progressive stasis taxonomy. One major danger is that the policy topics that interest teachers and students often turn out to be far too large to handle well once they are examined from the point of view of the stock issues. Furthermore, gun control, abortion, capital punishment, and the like are all chestnuts of national policy arguments that students are likely to choose if not warned away from them. Not that they are bad topics. They are just complex topics for which much relevant information and prior argumentation is available.

If students want to do thorough research into the studies about the possible deterrent effects of capital punishment, then they may well learn something although the resulting paper is almost certain to be a rehash of existing views rather than a useful contribution to the ongoing dialogue. But armchair arguments based on personal belief about whether capital punishment is a deterrent are of little value.

One solution is to modify the policy question at issue to allow the student to work on a related—and specifically current—topic, such as, "If capital punishment is to be used, is death by injection preferable to other modes?"

I have found it more successful, however, to limit my assignment of the policy essay to areas that my students either already have sufficient personal knowledge of, or are lacking only information that can be gained through a few interviews. That isn't easy. But I suggest that they consider one of the following situations, situations on which they are experts:

- a job you held;
- an organization you are or were a member of;
- your family;
- a course you took; or
- a regulation at your high school.

I then tell them to write the paper as a recommendation memo to a specific person or committee that actually has the power to consider the policy, such as the job supervisor, the school principal, the teacher, or the voting members of the club. Of course, I am a reader over the shoulder of the intended audience, so some matters that the audience would already be familiar with have to be explained in a bit more detail for my benefit (sometimes this is done in a separate author's memo). As it turns out, this extra detail rarely harms the paper; most deliberative bodies have to be reminded of how their own policies work before you can begin to persuade them to change the rules.

An excellent example of a solid policy recommendation written by students and in a real context is included in Caroline Eckhardt and David Stewart's text, *The Wiley Reader*. It is a report from a fraternity committee suggesting the need for significant changes in the organization's financial collection policy (266–70). It isn't exciting reading for a public audience, but then most policy argument is actually done within very precise rhetorical contexts, contexts that are nevertheless important to those involved.

Let me close this chapter with two real policy recommendations written by my students in response to the assignment discussed above. Since they are written as memos, they are untitled. The first is from the most recent advanced composition course I have taught:

> **TO:** **Mrs. Barb McCord, Head Secretary of Psychology and Special Education**
> **FROM:** **L. Diamond, Student Worker in Psychology and Special Education**
> **DATE:** **March 28, 1995**
> **RE:** **Work Request Policy**

As a student worker for the Psychology and Special Education Department, I submit to you the following Work Request Policy proposal.

At the moment, the Psychology and Special Education Department does not have a Work Request Policy, meaning that we do not have a policy that creates a standard, simple, and clear way for professors to turn in their work requests. Not having such a policy causes problems. For the year and a half that I have worked in this office, I have seen this problem grow. Instead of getting better, it is getting worse.

First of all, because there is not a set way or place to turn in work requests, the student worker office is cluttered with different stacks of things that need to be done. Some are piled by the computer, by the phone, and even under the table because they have been knocked off unknowingly. This disorganization causes many problems such as lost papers that need to be typed, or lost tests that have already been typed and dittoed.

Another problem is that, without a set way to turn in work requests, we do not always get complete directions such as when the project or task is needed by, who it is for, how many you need, whether the papers need to be stapled, and if so in what order. Once I stapled 130 packets that had eight pages. What I thought were answers for the students to choose from ended up being the answers to the test. This was realized about fifteen minutes before they were needed. The other student worker and I completed the task, and this turned out all right. However, there have been times when things did not get worked out. For example, it had been a busy day and a professor had left a ten page test for us to type. It did not have a date on it, so we did the other work that had to be done that day. So at about 1:30 the professor came in and asked why we had not typed his test, and that he needed it at 2:00. Needless to say, he did not get his test by the time he needed it and was very unhappy.

If the student workers were allowed to have the professors fill out a form called a Work Request form [see Figure 3], the professors' requests would be completed exactly how and when they wanted them. The student workers can draw this form, and ditto it ourselves. Then on the shelf by the professors' mail boxes we can set individual boxes that are labeled work request forms, ASAP, ditto, Type, errands, and miscellaneous. The individual boxes will keep things separated and more organized. The ASAP box will help us know exactly what needs to be done first, so we can immediately begin working on that task. All the professors would have to do is check the lines on the work request form that applied to their request, fill in their name and date, and if the professor has a special request, he can write this on the space provided on the form. (I have attached a sample form to the back.) Then they can put their requests in the appropriate box conveniently located by their mailboxes.

Also, on this form should be a space for student workers. This space would allow for student workers to write what disk the project is saved on and what name it is under. It will also allow student workers to know what has been done and what needs to be done. Then when the workers have completed a task, they will sign their names and file it. Then if there are problems, we can refer back to the forms to see who did that task and find out if it is saved on a disk so it can easily and quickly be corrected.

I talked to Frances Norman, the secretary of Elementary Education. She said that this form has worked well for them. She felt that before the work request forms, they had received many complaints, but since the form, they have had no complaints.

One problem that I can see with this policy would be the forms would use extra ink and paper. However, when you consider the amount of ink and paper that is wasted on projects that were done improperly, the ink and paper used for the forms will actually be less than what we are already using. The other problem that might occur is that the professors might not want to take the time to fill out the form, but when they see that it will save time because they will not have to explain their request over and over and it will stop mistakes that take up time to correct, they will realize that filling out the form will actually save them time.

This proposal is respectfully submitted for your consideration. As a student worker for the Psychology and Special Education Department, I would like you to seriously consider the Work Request Policy proposal, because I feel that it would be very beneficial for our department.

I like Leslie's proposal a lot. It handles all of the stock issues of a policy argument effectively, and since Leslie had interviewed someone

---

Psychology & Special Education Work Request

Instructor: _____

Date turned in: _____   Date needed _____

                                              Time needed _____

Instructions:

_____ type _____

_____ ditto _____

_____ collate/staple _____

_____ # of copies _____

_____ scantron key _____

Special Instruction _____

_____

_____

Work Report

Disk _____   Name of document: _____

Student Name	Procedure and or notes	Date/Time
_____	_____	_____
_____	_____	_____
_____	_____	_____
_____	_____	_____

Notes: _____

_____

_____

Figure 3. Student-designed work request form.

in another department that already had a similar procedure, her proposal demonstrates the sound use of an argument from analogy, an argument that allows Leslie to predict the future if the policy is adopted by the Psychology department. This is a revised final draft of her paper; before the final draft was submitted to me, the office manager had seen a copy, been persuaded, and instituted the policy. I am told it is working well.

My all-time favorite policy memo was actually written by an older returning student in an advanced writing class. My assignment happened to coincide with a policy concern she was already facing as volunteer director of a Big Brothers/Big Sisters organization in a nearby city. Normally, I hand out a copy of this piece as a model when I make the policy assignment. (Leslie had read and discussed it in class before writing her paper.)

TO: **Board of Directors, Big Brothers/Big Sisters of Lamar County**
FROM: **Beth O'Connor, Executive Director**
DATE: **August 1, 1982**
RE: **Recruitment Policy Revision**

As Executive Director of Big Brothers/Big Sisters of Lamar County I submit to you, the Board of Directors, the following recruitment policy.

During the last few months our office has been inundated with an overwhelming response from single-parents wanting to involve their children with Big Brothers/Big Sisters. This influx of new Little Brother/ Little Sister applications makes it essential that we deal with the immediate short-comings of our recruitment policy. We are faced with a major problem of too many applications from children and too few adult volunteers. Our current waiting list of active Little Brothers and Little Sisters stands at forty-five. Of these children, fifteen have been waiting for a Big Brother or Big Sister for over six months. As of today's date we have two prospective Big Sister applicants and one Big Brother applicant. This is a serious problem for our organization.

The psychological effect of being without a Big Brother/Big Sister match is a tragic one. The children who are the victims of single-parent homes are sensitive to rejection. When talking to those on the waiting list I consistently encounter a child expressing his or her condoning the unavailability of a Big Brother or Big Sister by commenting, "it doesn't really matter, he (she) probably wouldn't want to be around me anyhow." It is this negative self-degradation that must be avoided if we, as a Big Brother/Big Sister agency are to have a positive influence on the lives of these children.

Our program is based on the principle of caring and sharing. We have tried to involve mature, sensitive adults to work on a one to one basis with children from single-parent homes. We have used a person-to-person approach and appealed to the various civic organizations, churches, service clubs and schools to recruit our Big Brothers and Big Sisters. I propose that we continue these efforts and add a new, fresh approach for acquiring volunteers. The method would be a direct appeal to the community through the news media and I have tentatively given it the title of "One-to-One."

"One-to-One" would be based on a "Wednesday's Child" type public relations campaign. It would be modified to focus on the Big Brother/ Big Sister of Lamar County program. I contacted the Editor of the Paris News and the manager of radio station KPLT/KTXV. They have both volunteered "free" public service announcements. Their generosity relieves us of any financial burden on our approved or projected budgets.

A photograph of the "One-to-One" Little Brother or Little Sister would appear each Monday in the Paris News. They would also provide a 2" x 4" column with a special interest story. KPLT/KTXV would use "One-to-One" as the Monday 8:00 a.m., 9:00 a.m., noon, 5:00 p.m. and 6:00 p.m. lead-in for the news. This would be a 45 to 60 to 90 second promotion on the same Little Brother or Little Sister. The spot would be a, "meet Johnny, a cute seven year old boy who is waiting for you to volunteer to be his Big Brother" public interest story. The public service announcements would give the address and phone number of our Big Brother/Big Sister office. Once the prospective volunteer contacts our office we would use our required screening procedures, reference verifications, records check and trial period before matching the Big Brother/Big Sister.

I have spent several hours meeting with our agency's legal counselor going over the technicalities of this "public" approach for recruitment purposes. To avoid any legal problems we would have to have the consent of the managing conservator of the child. We would also want to have the enthusiastic agreement of the Little Brother/Little Sister whose name would be used in such a manner as to advertise their need for an adult friend. Our attorney has drawn up a separate consent form to be signed by all parties directly involved in the "One-to-One" program. Even though we will only be using their first names and a general personality-interest profile of the child we have included a space for the child to also sign. This goes one step further in allowing the Little Brother/Little Sister to be the main focus of "One-to-One."

As the idea of "One-to-One" began to formalize I felt it necessary to go beyond the legal aspects and consult our social service "team" for their input. Our foremost concern centered on the emotional ramifications of exposing the child's desire for adult companionship. Only one of the four social workers I approached was negative to the idea. She felt it would be using the children; making an example of them as being different; and that they might possibly be the brunt of negative peer pressure. It was her opinion that a public relations campaign such as this would exploit the child and would be detrimental to his or her emotional sense of well-being.

In order to respond to her objections I decided to discuss the possibility of such a program with a council of ten mothers whose children were on our waiting list. They were unanimous in their support for the proposed "One-to-One" program. After receiving their eager endorsement I visited with fifteen of their children and discussed the "possibility" of their being on the radio and having their picture in the paper. To say they were excited about the prospect would be an understatement.

I then formed an Advisory Committee consisting of four social workers, two psychologists, representatives from both the newspaper and the radio station, four mothers of Little Brothers and Little Sisters on our waiting list, the Planning Committee Chairman and our office staff. It was the consensus of our committee that I submit to you, on their behalf, the proposed "One-to-One" program as a necessary addition to our current recruitment program.

This proposal is respectfully submitted for your consideration. As Director of Big Brothers/Big Sisters of Lamar County it is my recommendation that this policy be adopted at the earliest possible date.

(*signed*)[8]

If you had been a member of the Board of Directors of Big Brothers/Big Sisters of Lamar County, how would you have voted?

9 A Useful Approach to Material Fallacies

Many college composition textbooks and some high school textbooks include sections devoted to teaching students certain argument types commonly identified as fallacious, presumably so that the students will avoid them in their own writing, and secondarily so that they will spot them in what they read. Unfortunately, these sections are rarely satisfactory.

The textbooks' sections are weak in four ways: in their definitions of fallacy itself, in their vague and overlapping descriptions of individual fallacies, in the exercises they include in which students are to identify fallacies, and in their failure to relate knowledge of fallacies to a student's writing.

The most common definition of fallacy—even in logic textbooks—is that a fallacy is an "error in argument." In addition to not being very helpful, that definition is misleading. To use the term "error" is to imply that the arguer made a mistake, a move he or she would not have made consciously—as I make "errors" in my checkbook. But fallacious arguments usually aren't "errors" in that sense. When someone points out an error in my checkbook, I immediately feel chagrined and agree that it is in fact an error and correct it. But when someone claims to see a fallacy in an argument, usually the arguer does not agree that it is one. In other cases, the arguer may agree that the argument shows weak reasoning but still decline to alter it. In this case, the "error" is *intentional.*

I prefer to define a fallacy, in general, as a "serious and identifiable defect in an argument." That definition isn't clear yet, but at least it allows for the possibility that the arguer can be aware of the fallacy and still be unwilling to change it. And including the qualifier "serious" in the definition means that there will be a number of borderline cases over which secondary argumentation will arise about whether the defect is serious enough to merit being designated a fallacy.

Fallacy theory, like most of logic, goes all the way back to Aristotle. Unfortunately, there has never been an agreed-upon definition or a usable classification of fallacies.

Howard Kahane, a leader in the informal logic movement, has taken a major step toward both classifying and defining fallacies through his discussion of three master fallacies. According to Kahane, there are three, and only three, broad ways in which an argument can be defective, that is, fallacious ("The Nature and Classification of Fallacies"):

1. An argument can be defective if it relies on premises that are questionable. In the Toulmin scheme, these can be either an unacceptable warrant or inaccurate data. Obviously, if the conclusion rests on the premises, and the premises are doubtful, then the argument isn't going to be acceptable. It's like building a house on a foundation of sand. No matter how much care is put into the house itself, the defective foundation—even though it may not be immediately obvious—makes it a bad house.

2. An argument can be defective if its premises are true but it fails to take into account other information (that is, other relevant premises) that would change the outcome. In the Toulmin scheme, this would mean a failure to consider a serious rebuttal condition. Suppose, for example, that someone made the following argument: "Since the average family income in this part of town is $45,000 a year, it is obviously an affluent neighborhood." That is an initially credible argument, assuming that the premise is accurate. But even if it is accurate, if there are twenty families in the neighborhood and one of them makes $700,000 a year while the others make under $11,000, then the failure to take this information into account makes the argument defective.

3. An argument can be defective if the formal relations between its premises and its conclusion violate any one of a number of rules of logic. This will be discussed at more length in Appendix B, but an example here will make the point: "This tree is a maple and it has leaves with five lobes. So all trees with five-lobed leaves are maples."

Kahane's three master fallacies can be immediately transformed into three questions one should ask of any argument after it has been analyzed carefully:

1. Are the premises—both explicit and implicit—acceptable?
2. Is all the relevant and important information taken into account?
3. Does the form of the argument satisfy the relevant rules of logic?

If the answer to all three questions is yes, then the argument is at least not fallacious, although it may still not be a good argument.

It is traditional as well as useful to separate discussion of ways that arguments can fail one of the first two questions from discussion of ways that they can fail on the third question. Arguments that fail on the grounds of the third question are deductive arguments that are formally fallacious; some of them are discussed in Appendix B. As I argued in Chapter 2, however, the distinction between induction and deduction is itself problematic. Furthermore, since real-life argumentation is rarely presented as formal deduction, we rarely need to understand formal fallaciousness in order to handle real texts. The difference between formally correct arguments and formally defective arguments is the substance of Logic with a capital L.

But arguments failing on one or both of Kahane's first two questions are usually described as being nonformally, or materially, fallacious. Extensive discussion of material fallacies is one of the hallmarks of the informal logic movement. Usually, when composition books include a list of common fallacies, material fallacies are meant.

I am going to call arguments that fail on question one or question two or both "substantive fallacies," since it is the substance of the premises that is unsatisfactory. The rest of this chapter, as well as the following one on statistical fallacies, will discuss and define some of the major types of substantive fallacies in a way that, I hope, makes them useful to writing teachers.

Fallacy theory has endured for several thousand years because a number of argument types are very common, very persuasive, and nevertheless defective. (But see Finocchiaro, who argues otherwise. Then see the responding articles by Govier; Jason; and Secor.) These arguments are not *obviously* defective. If they were, they would not be persuasive, nor would it be necessary to teach people about them.

Unfortunately, even the leading informal logic scholars differ about how many of such fallacies are important enough that people, including writers and writing teachers, need to be familiar with them. One current textbook designed for first-year argument courses discusses eighteen (Barnet and Bedau). Currently, the *St. Martin's Guide to Writing,* one of the most widely used textbooks for composition, lists fifteen (Axelrod and Cooper). The record apparently belongs to David Hackett Fischer, who lists 112 fallacies in the index to *Historians' Fallacies,* but he actually discusses and names more than that in the body of the book. The standard logic text in American colleges, Irving Copi and Carl Cohen's *Introduction to Logic* (9th ed.) lists only seventeen informal fallacies, dividing them into fallacies of relevance and fallacies of ambiguity.

In this chapter, I'm going to discuss eleven major fallacies (several with subtypes), selected on the grounds that in my experience, they are the ones that come up most often in discourse and are thus the ones most useful for writing teachers to understand.[9] And in the following chapter, I am going to discuss a group of fallacious uses of statistics. Here, again, a little knowledge is a dangerous thing. As I hope to show in the succeeding pages, the common material fallacies are more complicated than they are often made in textbooks. In fact, the textbook presentations are often contradictory and confusing to students. One is better off to know nothing of fallacies than to know them superficially. In most cases, as Booth and Gregory point out in the *Harper and Row Rhetoric*, fallacies and legitimate arguments exist in parallel pairs, which means that they are easily mistaken for each other. Often, deciding whether a given line of reasoning is fallacious or satisfactory becomes an occasion for complex secondary argumentation. Since even the informal logic experts have not found any satisfactory way to group these fallacies, I'm going to start with fallacies related to the GASCAP procedures, then move to several others of importance.

1. Hasty Generalization

As noted in earlier chapters, generalizing from limited data to a broader claim is one of the most common reasoning patterns, one that we all use every day. (The previous sentence may well be a hasty generalization itself.) Teachers observe a student in class for a few days and read one or two samples of his or her writing and generalize about the student's writing skills. Or teachers choose fifty test items out of the thousands that have been treated in a course and use those fifty for a measure of the student's knowledge. Or students learn of two instances in which a professor gave an F to a paper for being late and generalize that the professor is rigid and perhaps unfair. Or a principal observes a teacher in a classroom on two occasions and concludes that he is unable to maintain discipline. Or we hear a speaker once and conclude that she isn't any good. The list could go on.

In fact, most of the papers our students write involve generalizing of one sort or another. If a student writes about why she has chosen her major, she must generalize about both herself and the qualities the major requires (even though she has not come close to completing it yet) and will probably also generalize about the nature of the career it will lead to. If students write about high school dress codes or the cafeteria, the chances are great that they will generalize from their own experiences and perhaps those of a few friends. If a student compares some feature of high school and college, again he is generalizing on the basis of his experience with both high school and college. He may make claims based on his college history course that would not apply at all to some other section. And when students write literary interpretation, we expect them to generalize from a character's behavior or from a pattern of images.

There is, of course, nothing wrong with generalizing. We couldn't live without it. But generalizing from a sample of data rests on the assumption that remaining data, data we have *not* observed, will conform to what we have observed. Given the variability in human existence, that is obviously a dangerous assumption. But it isn't always wrong. Someone who eats three potato chips out of a bag and finds them all to be stiff and stale is more than justified in concluding that "the potato chips in this bag are stale," even though he or she has no direct knowledge of the great majority of the chips involved. Better yet, Ralph Johnson gives the illustration of tasting a spoonful of soup from a large cauldron; one spoonful is a good sample, assuming the soup has been well stirred ("Poll-ution" 164). As the spoonful-of-soup analogy also indicates, the commonsensical notion that one must have a larger sample for a larger target isn't, in fact, true: you don't need three spoonfuls from a cauldron three times as large.

The difficult question is, "When is a generalization hasty, and when is it satisfactory?" Obviously, generalizations do not actually fall into those two neat categories. Some are gross hasty generalizations, some are dubious generalizations, some are possibilities, some are well supported, and some are nearly certain. The best I can say is that when a generalization violates either the sufficiency or the typicality provisions of the STAR system, we can call the generalization hasty.

2. Poor Analogy

As explained in Chapter 4, reasoning by analogy means reasoning from a literally similar situation in another time or place and inferring that what occurred there would or should also occur in the situation under discussion. It is perhaps best considered as argument by precedent or parallel case. But whether an analogy is a poor one or not is itself a matter of argument. The soundness of the analogy rests on the extent of the similarities between the two situations and the lack of relevant dissimilarities. One can fairly easily fault an analogy by pointing out two relevant ways in which the situations differ.

Let me illustrate. At various times, East Texas State University has considered adding baseball to its list of intercollegiate sports. When that policy suggestion is made, a number of immediate negative results are instantly noted, the key ones being the expense and the many days of school baseball players must miss to play an NCAA schedule. Recently, one of our conference institutions did start playing baseball. So the argument was made by analogy that if Abilene Christian University can adopt baseball, we should be able to do it too. Both are small Texas schools which play in the NCAA Division II and in the Lone Star Conference.

But there the similarity ends. Abilene Christian is a primarily undergraduate institution (ETSU has 35 percent graduate students); ACU is a private school, not a state-funded one; and ACU sits in the middle of a city of more than 100,000, whose financial and team support can be drawn upon, while ETSU sits in a rural town of about 6,000 and rarely draws a crowd for athletics, even when its teams are nationally ranked. Those dissimilarities are enough to negate the analogy.

3. Fallible Sign

To the best of my knowledge, no book on logic or propaganda includes a fallacy of this name. So it may not be a particularly important misuse of argument. But if one can reason well from signs, then one can also reason badly. The obvious fallacy would be taking what Aristotle calls a "fallible" sign as if it were "infallible."

Until recently, it was common for some store chains to make prospective employees pass a lie detector test before hiring them. Eventually, the practice was challenged in the courts, and a ruling was handed down that the practice was illegally discriminatory because lie detectors did not provide accurate enough signs of a person's real behavior. (Of course, the results of lie detector tests had been rejected in law courts before this.) Similarly, there are various reasons for doubting the accuracy of the simpler tests of intoxication, so Breathalyzer™ tests are not used for proof; instead, a blood alcohol test is required. And how often do we see signs of cheating in a student's work, signs that we would be properly afraid to draw a strong conclusion from?

And finally, let's consider some of the famous "deductions" of Sherlock Holmes. In the beginning of "The Blue Carbuncle," Holmes is examining a "very seedy and disreputable hard felt hat, much the worse for wear, and cracked in several places." It was dropped by a man who also dropped a Christmas goose with a tag on it saying, "for Mrs. Henry Baker." Since the hat contains the initials H.B., the police assume that the owner of the hat is a Mr. Henry Baker. But there are many Henry Bakers in London, and Holmes has been asked to see what he can determine that may help the police locate the proper Henry Baker.

After Watson has looked at the hat and confessed he can tell nothing about the owner, Holmes takes over:

> ". . . It is perhaps less suggestive than it might have been," he remarked, "and yet there are a few inferences which are very distinct, and a few others which represent at least a strong balance of probability. That the man was highly intellectual is of course obvious on the face of it, and also that he was fairly well-to-do within the last three years, although he has now fallen upon evil days. He had foresight, but has less now than formerly, pointing to a moral retrogression, which, when taken with the decline of his fortunes, seems to indicate some evil influence, probably drink at work. This may account also for the obvious fact that his wife has ceased to love him." . . .
>
> "He has, however, retained some degree of self-respect. He is a man who leads a sedentary life, goes out little, is out of training entirely, is middle-aged, has grizzled hair which he has cut within the last few days, and which he anoints with lime-cream. These are the more patent facts which are to be deduced from his hat. Also, by the way, that it is extremely improbable that he has gas laid on in his house." (Doyle 152)

Watson, baffled, asks for clarification from Holmes about several of the conclusions, in succession:

> ". . . I am unable to follow you. For example, how did you deduce that this man was intellectual?"
>
> For answer Holmes clapped the hat upon his head. It came right over the forehead and settled upon the bridge of his nose. "It is a question of cubic capacity," said he: "a man with so large a brain must have something in it."
>
> "The decline of his fortunes, then?"
>
> "This hat is three years old. These flat brims curled at the edge came in then. It is a hat of the best quality. Look at the band of ribbed silk and the excellent lining. If this man could afford to buy so expensive a hat three years ago, and he has had no hat since, then he has assuredly gone down in the world."
>
> "Well, that is clear enough, certainly. But how about the foresight, and the moral retrogression?"
>
> Sherlock Holmes laughed. "Here is the foresight," said he, putting his finger upon the little disc and loop of the hat-securer. "They are never sold upon hats. If this man ordered one, it is a sign of a certain amount of foresight, since he went out of his way to take this precaution against the wind. But since we see that he has broken the elastic, and has not troubled to replace it, it is obvious that he has less foresight now than formerly, which is a distinct proof of a weakening nature. On the other hand, he has endeavoured to conceal some of these stains upon the felt by daubing them with ink, which is a sign that he has not entirely lost his self-respect."
>
> "Your reasoning is certainly plausible."
>
> "The further points, that he is middle-aged, that his hair is grizzled,

that it has recently been cut, and that he uses lime-cream, are all to be gathered from a close examination of the lower part of the lining. The lens discloses a large number of hair ends, clean cut by the scissors of the barber. They all appear to be adhesive, and there is a distinct odor of lime-cream. This dust, you will observe, is not the gritty grey dust of the street, but the fluffy brown dust of the house, showing that it has been hung up indoors most of the time; while the marks of moisture upon the inside are proof positive that the wearer perspired very freely, and could, therefore, hardly be in the best of training.

"But his wife—you said that she has ceased to love him."

"This hat has not been brushed for weeks. When I see you, my dear Watson, with a week's accumulation of dust upon your hat, and when your wife allows you to go out in such a state, I shall fear that you also have been unfortunate enough to lose your wife's affections."

"But he might be a bachelor."

"Nay, he was bringing home the goose as a peace-offering to his wife. Remember the card upon the bird's leg."

"You have an answer to everything. But how on earth do you deduce that the gas is not laid on in his house?"

"One tallow stain, or even two, might come by chance; but, when I see no less than five, I think that there can be little doubt that the individual must be brought into frequent contact with burning tallow—walks upstairs at night probably with his hat in one hand and a guttering candle in the other. Anyhow, he never got tallow stains from a gas jet. Are you satisfied?"

"Well, it is very ingenious," said I, laughing. . . . (152–54)

Holmes, of course, turns out to be correct in all his surmises, but as my students quickly point out when prompted, his reasoning from the various signs he sees in the hat is actually anything but solid, beginning with his totally unacceptable assumption that a person with a large hat size must be intelligent and going on through the argument that anyone wearing such a hat must have fallen on hard times. My students point out that it could be an old hat he kept for knockaround wear in bad weather, or a hat he had found, or a disguise, etc. And despite Holmes's reasoning, the wearer could be a bachelor taking a goose to his mother or sister, or he could be a widower. Or he might be a husband with a loving wife who doesn't, even in Victorian London, feel responsible for brushing his hat. (This illustration has been adapted from Levi 6–14.)

4. *Post Hoc*

Post hoc arguments are faulty causal arguments in which, since two events correlate with each other in time, the arguer asserts a cause-and-effect relationship between them. In identifying such arguments, it's helpful to keep in mind the meaning of the whole Latin phrase from which the argument gets its name: *post hoc, ergo propter hoc.* The phrase means "after the fact, therefore because of the fact." And that is an exact description of the premise/conclusion shape of the fallacy. The premise is that event A closely followed or follows event B in time. The conclusion is always a causal statement: "So B must have caused A."

Again, such reasoning is common, and it mimics the legitimate causal reasoning discussed earlier. If we eat an unusual dish at a new Mexican restaurant and develop stomach pains two hours later, we are likely to leap to at least the tentative conclusion that the dish caused the stomach problems. We could, of course, be quite wrong. We might have been already coming down with the stomach flu. If we ate the same dish on three occasions and got pains several hours later on all three occasions, we would be much more likely to conclude that eating the dish caused the pain. And in this case, few of us would regard such reasoning as fallacious. That's why the *post hoc* fallacy is so seductive; it is only a slight perversion of real causal reasoning.

Colleges and college professors aren't above using the *post hoc* fallacy when it suits their purposes. We all know the statistics which show that college graduates, on the average, earn higher salaries than noncollege graduates. The data are clear that the higher salaries follow the degrees in time. And it is so seductively easy to assume that the degree caused the higher salary. But we don't know that to be the case. Quite possibly, the mental and personal traits of the student, the ones that caused her to succeed in college, might really be the cause, and she would have been able to work her way up to such a salary without college—especially since she would have had four or more extra years to do it.

Another interesting and real example occurs in lawsuits alleging discrimination in the workplace. It is often easy enough to show that a class of workers—say women or an ethnic minority—earn lower average salaries or hold fewer managerial positions. And that often seems to show that the company must have discriminated (we have causal reasoning by sign here). But lawyers for the company would argue that some other factor explains the chronological correlation. For example, the women may have lower salaries but also fewer years' experience with the company. Or the ethnic minority may have lower levels of education, which would tend to account for lower rates of promotion, etc. Major legal battles are now being fought over just what the standards of proof of discrimination shall be and who bears the burden of proof, the employer or the injured party.

The following paragraph appeared in a letter to the editor of the East Texas State University campus newspaper. It thus has the virtue here of being a real rather than a constructed example and of (perhaps) being representative of student writing. It will also allow me to make several points about two of the fallacies discussed so far. I will number the propositions for ease of reference:

> [1] Since Commerce was voted wet, the town and the University have gone downhill. [2] Enrollment at the school and [3] population of the town have decreased. [4] Liquor sales haven't made this town and University, all they have done is help *destroy it.*

The student argues that [2] declining enrollment and [3] declining population prove "the town and the University have gone downhill." Such an argument rests on at least two closely related, unstated assumptions: "Bigger is better" and "To lose population is to go downhill." Using the tests based on Kahane's three master fallacies, one might well regard that portion of the argument as resting on highly questionable premises. Many universities deliberately seek ways to reduce enrollment, and presumably they do not believe that they are "going downhill." However, anyone familiar with the context would know that ETSU was not attempting to reduce enrollment at this time, but was in fact attempting to increase it.

This portion of the argument can also be reasonably described as a hasty generalization. The student has looked at one sample of data, population, and generalized to the overall quality of life of the town and the university. Surely, other matters should be involved in a generalization that both the town and the university have "gone downhill." (This could also be seen as reasoning from the fallible sign of population growth.)

In addition, the writer—having "shown" that life has gone "downhill" after the vote to sell liquor—then concludes in [4] that the election caused the decline. The only evidence for the causal claim is the chronological proximity. And that isn't enough. Even if readers agreed that the town had gone downhill, they would not need to accept the causal claim being made. It would only be a reasonable argument by Mill's method of difference if nothing else relevant to the town's "decline" changed.

Often, English texts use passages like this one in exercises in which students are asked to decide whether the passage is fallacious and, if it is, to name the fallacy. Such exercises are dangerous for several reasons. First, the different fallacies have rarely been defined with much precision. Second, relationships between various fallacies have rarely been explained. And third, as my discussion of the letter on the Commerce wet/dry election illustrates, many real fallacies can be named in several ways, depending on how the argument itself is analyzed and on what unstated premises are supplied.

Every *post hoc* argument is also a hasty generalization of a special kind, a hasty causal generalization. Thus a student would be correct in identifying the argument about the new Mexican dish and the stomach pains as a *post hoc* argument or as a hasty generalization. But I know of no text that explains this connection. And many cause/effect claims are argued indirectly from signs, so the fallacy could be either *post hoc* or *argument from fallible sign*. Such exercises often become tests of ingenuity more than of a student's sense of reasonableness in argument: the real problem becomes figuring out "what answer did the textbook writer want me to give?" Teachers, armed with answer manuals, would do well to work the exercises themselves first and then to see how close they come to the answers in the manual. Even that isn't foolproof since teachers tend to be fairly good at figuring out what answer was wanted by a test question.

If I saw the sample paragraph about Commerce included in a name-that-fallacy exercise, I would know that the writer wanted me to spot a *post hoc* fallacy, but I should not assume that my students have that same sense—especially where more confusing examples are involved. (For more about the *post hoc* fallacy, see Walton, *Informal Logic* 212–22.)

5. *Argumentum ad Verecundiam*

Six common substantive fallacies have been given Latin names beginning with *argumentum ad*. They include the *argumentum ad baculum* (argument with a bludgeon); the *argumentum ad hominem* (to be discussed below); the *argumentum ad misericordiam* (to be discussed below); the *argumentum ad verecundiam* (usually called "false authority"); the *argumentum ad ignorantiam* (the argument from ignorance: "You can't prove there aren't any flying saucers, so they exist"); and the *argumentum ad populum* (to be discussed below).[10] Sometimes these Latin names are taken to imply the great antiquity of the fallacy analysis. Actually, three of these fallacies were named by John Locke in "An Essay Concerning Human Understanding" (1690). We don't know where the other three got their names, but they do not come from classical times.

In some senses the fallacy of false authority needs little explanation. It occurs when someone argues by authority (from the GASCAP schema) and uses as the source a person or persons who are not well qualified or who have a known bias. It can also occur when an arguer takes the citing of one or even a few authorities as settling an issue.

On many issues about which we must hold positions, we cannot investigate the relevant data ourselves: the effects of school busing to achieve integration, the value of building a space station or a superconducting super collider, the cost of reconstructing four blocks of city streets, the effect of adding more insulation to our houses, or what medicine to take for a disease; these are obvious examples.

So we consult the experts, either in person or in print. The problem lies largely in determining who is an expert and then making sure we do not cite as relevant authorities people who are not. However, it is easy to cite people who sound authoritative but are not, and when this is done, we have the fallacious citation of authority.

The traditional name, *argumentum ad verecundiam,* doesn't reflect the fallacy at all. Locke bestowed the name to designate arguments which "allege the opinions of men whose parts, learning, eminency, power, or some other cause has gained a name and settled their reputation in the common esteem with some kind of authority" (Locke, quoted in Hamblin 159). *Verecundia* means "shame" or "shyness" in Latin, and the name was used because, "When men are established in any kind of dignity, it is thought a breach of modesty for others to derogate any way from it, and question the authority of men who are in possession of it" (Locke, quoted in Hamblin 160). It isn't clear whether Locke considered all such arguments as fallacious, and Hamblin remarks that "[h]istorically speaking, argument from authority has been mentioned in lists of valid argument-forms as often as in lists of Fallacies" (43). That seems entirely appropriate to me. There is nothing fallacious about basing an argument on a good authority. Of course, such an argument will not be definitive since other equally good authorities may believe differently or because even the consensus of all authorities could still be wrong. Arguments from authority can be better or worse, and the addition of further evidence can modify the strength with which the conclusion can be held.

Some analysts, such as Copi (*Introduction to Logic* 6th ed. 106), cite advertisements in which sports or entertainment figures recommend a product unconnected to their fields as simple illustrations of fallacious citation of authority. Roger Staubach, Annapolis graduate, former star quarterback for the Dallas Cowboys, and football Hall of Fame member, used to sell Rolaids on television. I think it's appropriate to study the psychological technique of identifying a product with a recognized and presumably admired public figure (and I treat this, below, as a version of the *argumentum ad populum*), but as I read the TV ads, Staubach is not being cited as an authority on Rolaids, any more than Joe Namath was claimed to be an authority on pantyhose. Staubach is simply a spokesperson for the product—someone who was chosen, no doubt, for his own image in hopes that it would rub off onto the product.

Whenever we get information about factual matters at second hand, the source can be placed somewhere on a continuum of credibility that includes at least the following levels:

- Rumor—no specific source, someone had heard X.
- Hearsay—Joe told me that he had X from Mike.
- Eyewitness—Joe was there, and he told me X.
- Corroborated eyewitness—Joe was there and told me X, which Mike and Tom have corroborated.
- Mechanically recorded—videotape or audiotape or film.
- Historically validated—enough corroborative data that the material is accepted in standard reference sources.

Now anyone who has done research into the facts of, say, an author's life or the dates on which historic events happened knows that even major reference sources can be wrong, just as a contemporary news account in a reputable newspaper can be.

More often, we use authorities, not to give us facts, but to give us judgments based either on their own research findings or on their supposedly widespread knowledge of their field. Here is the most fertile ground for the growth of fallacious citation. And here, too, a hierarchy of possible levels of authoritativeness exists:

- Unnamed experts say X.
- A famous person says X, but X is not related to the field he or she is famous in.
- Someone involved with the subject, either by profession or as an avocation, testifies in an interview.
- Someone involved with the subject, either by profession or as an avocation, testifies in print.
- Someone involved with the subject, either by profession or as an avocation, testifies in print in a journal refereed by other specialists.
- A specialist in the field, respected by other specialists, testifies.
- A specialist in the field, respected by other specialists, testifies and is corroborated by other specialists.

There are many problems with making any use of this hierarchy, especially where composition students are concerned. If a student finds a view in print somewhere by an author who at least has some experience in a field, the student tends to accept the information as authoritative. We can scarcely expect the student to know whether Professor Plomp, who teaches at a prestigious university and has a doctorate in the field, is regarded by other professors as an eccentric addlebrain holding laughable pet theories or is a genuinely respected scholar. As I write this, John Mack, a respected Harvard professor of psychology, a Pulitzer Prize winner, has just published a lengthy book, *Abduction: Human Encounters with Aliens,* in which he argues that the stories of being kidnapped by aliens are often true. The scientific community and most psychologists think the book is absurd. Who is the "expert"? (See Monaghan.)

We can hardly expect students to distinguish between reputable journals and less prestigious ones. Moreover, we can rarely expect students to make subtle discriminations between such authorities' expert testimony as to the findings of their discipline and their human testimony about what public policies we ought therefore to adopt. The nuclear scientist is crucial in telling us what the effects of building nuclear power plants will be, but she is no more an expert than anyone else at deciding whether these effects are ultimately acceptable.

In classical rhetoric, according to Corbett, a speaker's *ethos* was as crucial to persuasion as *logos* or *pathos* (93). And one way to evaluate expert testimony is to say that an expert must manifest the three classical traits necessary to ethos: good sense, good character, and good will. *Good sense* in this context means both having the necessary knowledge and being able to reason well. *Good character* means being known for telling the truth. And *good will* means having the audience's interests, rather than some personal advantage, as the objective.

But, again, problems arise in using these standards to determine when an appeal to authority is fallacious, especially where students are concerned. To determine whether the source has "good sense," the auditor has to know a good deal about reasoning in general as well as about the field involved. And we go to experts precisely because we are not ourselves knowledgeable about the field. Determining whether the authority is knowledgeable is especially difficult if people do only brief research, for in this case they will not read widely enough to find out whether the expert in question is widely published, widely cited by others, widely corroborated by others. Without such information, researchers have almost no way of judging the writer's expertise or the writer's reputation for "good character." Critical readers learn to look for some textual criteria: explanation of the research the judgment is based on, careful qualifications on the judgment, acknowledgment of exceptions to it, attention to counterarguments. But it would take a good deal of teaching to expect students to become able to discriminate between the credible text and the dubious one. We are back to Toulmin's notion of evaluation as field dependent.

On the issue of "good will," it's ironic that we usually reject authorities if they have a vested interest in the view they assert, such as doctors who are employed by the American Tobacco Institute to attack studies connecting smoking to lung cancer or a lobbyist for the American Tariff League testifying on the economic benefits of tariffs. Citing such an authority is usually held to be fallacious since the "authority" does not have our best interests at heart, yet those who reject an authority on such grounds must be careful that they do not themselves engage in the fallacy of circumstantial *ad hominem* (discussed below). If the expert gives an argument—as opposed to giving only expert opinion—then it is fallacious to reject the argument merely because of his or her circumstances. And yet, most of us *feel* that such arguments are at least suspect. Because of special circumstances, might the expert be inclined to omit other relevant information from the argument, information that he or she would be aware of but that would not serve the cause and that we could not be expected to know?

Kahane points out that fallacious citations of authority tend to fall into the broad master fallacy category of "questionable premise" since we usually cite authorities to provide some grounds for an argument we wish to make, for example, psychiatric testimony in a law court to argue that the accused should not be imprisoned because the experts say he suffers from a psychological problem and was not responsible for his actions.

Kahane also sums up the differences between fallacious and acceptable citations of authority as follows:

> [R]oughly speaking, an appeal to another person or source is proper (not fallacious) when we're reasonably sure that this "authority" has the knowledge or judgment we need, we can expect the authority to tell the truth, *and* we don't have the time, inclination, or ability to form an expert opinion of our own. (*Logic and Contemporary Rhetoric* 48)[11]

6. Accident

Logicians commonly name the misapplication of a general principle as the *fallacy of accident*. When the fallacy occurs, someone uses the general principle as a warrant without noticing the rebuttal conditions by which it is limited. Examples include arguments which assume that freedom of speech is unlimited or which ignore the "special" status of a person involved (e.g., "diplomatic immunity"). A common illustration involves the warrant that "you can put out a fire by throwing water on it," a warrant which leads to fallacious reasoning if one is dealing with a gasoline fire. Toulmin, Rieke, and Janik give the example of a doctor who generally prescribes penicillin for upper-respiratory infections, on the warrant that the drug usually is effective with them. If that warrant is applied to a patient with the special status of having a penicillin allergy, however, it becomes fallacious.

7. *Argumentum ad Populum*

Most of the fallacies with Latin names are fairly well defined, but the *argumentum ad populum* is not. For example, in a very fine composition textbook, Adelstein and Pival say that

> *Ad populum* is an appeal "to the people"—particularly to their prejudices or fears—rather than to the merits of the issue. A politician who exploits the racial hostility generated in a community over an explosive busing issue is guilty of this fallacy. The unscrupulous salesman who uses a "hoopla" campaign to stimulate an emotional response toward a product is also guilty of *ad populum*. (389)

No one is likely to defend a politician who "exploits" racial hostility since racial hostility is an acknowledged prejudice and "exploitation" is evil by definition. But would we say the same thing of a politician who argued for arms reduction and "made use of" (not "exploited") our fears of a nuclear war? Would we say a university was guilty of fallacious argument if it engaged in a vigorous campaign (not "hoopla") to encourage enrollment and based part of that campaign on the populace's prejudice against ignorance and unemployment?

The qualifying phrase "rather than to the merits of the issue" is important. It presumes that somehow an issue has merits of its own separable from the fears of the audience. It also makes the act of appealing to the audience's fears or prejudices or common beliefs fallacious only when the appeal is made by itself. This hedge in the definition is common. Gerald Levin says that "when an appeal is made to the biases of the audience as a substitute for presenting facts and reasons, we describe such a fallacious appeal as an *ad populum* argument" (202). And Ronald Munson says, "The *ad populum* fallacy is committed by appealing to a group's prejudices and attitudes rather than to relevant reasons and evidence" (271).

So here we apparently have a mode of argument which (1) is fallacious when it appears by itself but apparently becomes legitimate when accompanied by other arguments; (2) is defined by presuming that a clear difference exists between appealing to a group's attitudes and to relevant reasons and evidence; and (3) would, awkwardly, include such supposedly separate arguments as the *ad hominem* and the *ad misericordiam.* I submit that every attempt to make a value argument must include as part of its "reasons and evidence" precisely the group's attitudes. If one is trying to persuade the voters in a city that a particular parcel of land should not be rezoned to allow a health club to be built on it, the attitudes toward health clubs and businesses of the populace in general and especially of the citizens living near the parcel are certainly part of the relevant argument.

Frankly, that sort of definition isn't very helpful to precise analysis. It tends to end up with analysts criticizing emotional arguments they dislike as "mere *ad populum* appeals to prejudice" and praising emotional arguments they approve of as "carefully adapted to the dominant values of the audience." Such "analysis" is, in fact, name-calling by the analyst.

As I see it, we might be able to make more headway toward defining the illegitimate *ad populum* by looking at a complex of specific devices that constitute it, although I know of no specialist in informal logic who has used this approach. In October of 1937, a group of American scholars, concerned about several social movements in the U.S. and Hitler's rise to power in Germany, formed the Institute for Propaganda Analysis. It is not very widely known today, but several of its terms for specific propaganda techniques have come down to us and are often included in lists of material fallacies.

The institute had a good deal of trouble defining *propaganda.* Although the term has severely negative overtones, there has never been a successful way to distinguish arguments that are propaganda from others that are not. Frequently "propaganda" seems to mean "the other side's arguments." The institute ended up defining propaganda as

> an expression of opinion or action by individuals or groups, deliberately designed to influence opinions or actions of other individuals or groups with reference to pre-determined ends. (Miller 13)

That definition includes nearly all value or policy arguments—whether fallacious or not—but nevertheless could be read as excluding a good many arguments, scientific, historical, etc., all of those whose conclusions might be called "descriptive" as opposed to "evaluative." In addition to being broadly inclusive, the definition does not itself involve any evaluation. That is, for the institute, propaganda includes both good arguments and bad ones, and both should be carefully analyzed. The institute made this view explicit: "Socially desirable propaganda will not suffer from such examination, but the opposite type will be detected and revealed for what it is" (Miller 23). I'm not sure what the last phrase means: Revealed to be propaganda? Revealed to be undesirable? Perhaps revealed to be fallacious?

The Institute for Propaganda Analysis, however, had the same problem that many later analysts do. They didn't seem able to stick with their own definition. Later that same pamphlet asks, "What is the chief danger of propaganda? It appeals to emotion, and decisions made under stress of emotion often lead to disaster when the emotion crowds out cool, dispassionate thought" (Miller 26). Now if there is socially desirable propaganda, it makes no sense to assume that propaganda is inherently dangerous.

And when the institute reached its major contribution, a list of what it decided were the seven common propaganda devices, each involved fallacious argument (see Lee and Lee). It's hard to see how fallacious argument could be socially valuable and stand up to close analysis.

Although the Institute for Propaganda Analysis is largely forgotten, its seven common propaganda devices have filtered into the common lists of material fallacies, so that far more people have heard of them than of the institute. The original seven were

- The Name Calling Device
- The Glittering Generalities Device
- The Transfer Device
- The Testimonial Device
- The Plain Folks Device
- The Card Stacking Device
- The Band Wagon Device (Miller 27)

It would clarify matters and perhaps prove ultimately useful if we now defined the fallacy of *argumentum ad populum* as the use of one or more of these seven devices. Discussing each one briefly will show how each, indeed, appeals to a popularly held prejudice and substitutes emotion for argument. "Name-calling" attempts to create a negative judgment of anything by tagging it with a name the audience already has negative reactions to. A sex-education textbook is bad because it is "pornography." A politician is bad because he's "liberal" (obviously, one uses this fallacy with careful awareness of the audience; what is a pejorative term to one group may not be to another). Medicare is bad because it's "socialistic," and a "civil rights" bill promoting "affirmative action" is bad because it's a "quota" bill. This fallacy is now sometimes called the *fallacy of scare words*. It's important that the words being used to attack the position in question be essentially emotional and undefined.

Glittering generalities are "Name Calling in reverse" (Lee and Lee 48). The only difference is that the terms tied to the person or proposal or product being argued about evoke a highly positive response in the audience, again without any precise definition, e.g., "modern." (Some people confuse "hasty generalization" with "glittering generalities," but the two are quite different.) In advertising, terms like "smooth," "natural," "new," "scientific," and "fresh" are common generalities that glitter. Similar terms can be found in any prep school brochure or college catalog, in many letters of recommendation, on menus, and in mail-order catalogs.

These two types of *ad populum* appeals correspond to what some semanticists call *snarl words* and *purr words*. Richard Weaver called them "god words" and "devil words" (212, 222).

"*Transfer* is a device by which the propagandist carries over the authority, sanction, and prestige of something we respect and revere to something he would have us accept" (Miller 30). Instead of endowing the subject involved with negative or positive traits adjectivally, the arguer associates the subject with some other noun or icon which the audience values, such as the church, the Statue of Liberty, or the flag. Again, the "argument" is made by association rather than by propositional claims.

The device called *testimonial* by the Institute for Propaganda Analysis simply involves getting someone the audience views positively to endorse the product or position. It is the standard advertiser's technique of having a Hollywood star sell orange juice.

The *plain folks* device is a very restricted fallacy, if it is a fallacy at all, in which a politician or other public figure attempts to gain our support or acceptance by behaving publicly in ways that "show" he or she is really just an ordinary person like the rest of us. I'm not sure whether being photographed eating pizza or a taco during a political campaign constitutes a fallacy, but if a politician campaigning in a rural district deliberately puts on overalls that he never wears otherwise and adopts a regional dialect or chews tobacco on purpose for the occasion, many people would say that such false image making is a fallacious attempt to appeal to the audience's emotions. Image creating is certainly part of politics, but with the growth of mass communications, I don't think we see much of the "plain folks" appeal.

Card stacking is simply the use of carefully selected evidence for a position and the ignoring of other relevant evidence that isn't so favorable. It thus corresponds to Kahane's master fallacies of using questionable premises and ignoring other relevant evidence.

Finally, the *bandwagon* device appeals to the natural human inclination to behave in ways that make us seem to fit in rather than be separated from our peers. The bandwagon argument uses as a premise that "lots of people are doing it" and concludes that "it's the right thing to do" or "you should do it too." It is the classic argument of every teenager seeking permission to stay out later or to wear the newest bizarre fashion. And it is the argument of every ad based on how popular the product or company already is. Logically, we know that "everybody does it" or "a lot of people do it" is not an adequate premise for "therefore you should do it too." In fact, such an argument relies on the unstated warrant that "whatever is commonly done is good," a questionable premise if ever there was one. Arguments based on appeals to tradition ("We have always done it this way" or "We have always believed X") are variations of the same pattern; the group which has jumped on the bandwagon is merely spread out through time.

A closing caution: not all appeals to common prejudices are fallacious. After all, the argument that many people are starving and that therefore it is good for us to give to charities which help them is based on our "common prejudice" that starving is bad and that there is a common bond between humans that makes helping the unfortunate desirable.

8. *Argumentum ad Misericordiam*

Every college teacher is familiar with the student who, near the end of the term, argues,

> This has really been a rough semester for me. I've tried very hard in your class, but I'm also working two jobs to support my two children. I'm a single parent and I've had trouble finding babysitters. And then I got very sick for three weeks and couldn't attend class. So even though I have a lot of absences and failed the two tests and turned in only half of the required papers, won't you please give me at least a C? I really did learn a lot.

High school teachers face variations of the same plea, including those from students who have been too busy with athletics to keep up their grades.

That is a fairly typical instance of the fallacy called *argumentum ad misericordiam*, the appeal to pity, which can be defined as "using sympathy to advance a contention" (Barry 298). Apparently, appealing to pity is illogical because pity is an emotion, and appealing to emotions in a discourse is part of pathos rather than logos or even ethos. But if that were the case, the appeal to pity would not be a fallacy because it would not be part of the argument, the logos, at all. And there is clearly nothing wrong with a discourse manifesting emotion and attempting to arouse emotions in the auditor as well.

Perhaps we can clarify by saying that when an arguer uses the appeal to the audience's pity in place of arguing for a conclusion, then the failure to argue the point while still asking for its acceptance is fallacious. This has the awkwardness of making a fallacy of something that in one sense isn't an argument at all. On the other hand, if the arguer has claimed that somehow the premises about the sad plight of a person or group do lead to some conclusion, then he has at least claimed an argument, and the argument is unsound.

But the notion of an appeal to pity being fallacious needs further clarification. We hear many arguments daily that appeal to our sense of pity, pity for a person or group which has somehow been shortchanged by existence. When we are told of the horrors of the Nazi prison camps as part of an argument both for the evils of the Nazi regime and for an understanding of the camp survivors, we do not feel that this is fallacious. When the horrors of back-street abortions were discussed prior to *Roe v. Wade*, few people felt that these horrors were illegitimate arguments (although many felt and still do that they were not decisive). And when today we are shown the human agonies in Bosnia, we do not feel that these appeals to our emotions are necessarily fallacious.

The point is that sometimes appeals to pity (or other emotions) as premises to arguments are legitimate and sometimes they are not. We need a definition of *argumentum ad misericordiam* that distinguishes between the two situations. Otherwise, and this is common, students who have been taught that there is such a fallacy see any emotional piece of discourse as fallacious. (One corresponding result can be that their own writing becomes dry and unemotional, ignoring the classical injunction that to be effective, discourse needs all three types of "proofs": logos, pathos, and ethos.)

I propose the following view: an argument involving an appeal to pity in a premise is fallacious if, and only if, the premise is logically unrelated to the claim made in the conclusion. No doubt the premise will be related to the conclusion somehow. Otherwise, the argument would not persuade. But often, the only relation is that the premise and the conclusion share a term. In the argument with which I opened this section, the premises can be summed up as

> Student X has endured an abnormally painful semester through no fault of his own.

The conclusion drawn from it seems to be

> Student X should receive at least a C.

Clearly, the two propositions share the term "Student X." But to determine whether the appeal to pity in the premise leads to a fallacy, one needs to examine the argument with the Toulmin model, identify the unstated warrant, and ask whether the warrant is at all credible. In this argument, the unstated warrant apparently is

> All students enduring abnormally painful semesters through no fault of their own should receive at least C's.

But how could one provide backing for such a principle? Given our concept of what grades are supposed to mean, the warrant seems clearly indefensible to me. Now if the student had used the same set of facts as premises and drawn a conclusion saying, "I should be given extra time to complete my assignments," then the unstated assumption would be, "All students who have abnormally difficult semesters through no fault of their own should be allowed special considerations in completing their work." I may not agree with that warrant, but it seems credible.

A clearer example. The fallacy of *argumentum ad misericordiam* is often illustrated with a lawyer's arguing for finding his client not guilty because the client is in some way worthy of being pitied. Several logic texts cite the following speech used by Clarence Darrow in defending Thomas Kidd, an officer of the Amalgamated Woodworkers Union. Kidd had been indicted for criminal conspiracy:

> I appeal to you not for Thomas Kidd, but I appeal to you for the long line—the long, long line reaching back through the ages and forward to the years to come—the long line of despoiled and downtrodden people of the earth. I appeal to you for those men who rise in the morning before daylight comes and who go home at night when the light has faded from the sky and give their life,

their strength, their toil to make others rich and great. I appeal to
you in the name of those women who are offering up their lives
to this modern god of gold, and I appeal to you in the name of
those little children, the living and the unborn. (Copi, *Introduction to Logic* 6th ed. 102–3)

Kidd was found not guilty (although we cannot conclude that the
jury's finding was the result of the above speech; to do so would be to
commit a *post hoc* fallacy). Nevertheless, most argument analysts would
agree that Darrow had engaged in fallacious reasoning, since the sympathy evoked for the labor movement in general had no logical connection to whether Kidd had engaged in a criminal conspiracy. (I'll have
more to say about this case below, however.)

But if after the accused is found guilty, the lawyer is arguing about
the sentence to be assessed, then—it seems to me—some personal appeal to pity involving the circumstances of the defendant and his or her
family might well become relevant. The unstated warrant then becomes
something like "people who are suffering greatly and on whom others
depend should sometimes be given lenient sentences." I do not necessarily accept that warrant, but I do not find it obviously untenable. In
this case, I would say the appeal to pity is not fallacious, but that does
not make the lawyer's argument decisive either.

A final example: we are all familiar with the magazine advertisements that picture a malnourished and poorly dressed child, with accompanying text about the poverty of the region or ethnic group he or
she represents. Clearly, our emotions, specifically our pity for the help-
less child, are being appealed to. In my experience, students who have
studied the *argumentum ad misericordiam* as it is usually presented do
not hesitate to label such ads fallacious. I can argue the evaluation either way. Since the conclusion is likely to be that "you, the reader, should
send money to help this starving child," one could say the child's condition is logically irrelevant to the conclusion, for the only connection
would lie in the unstated warrant that "the reader has a moral duty to
help all children who are starving." Such an assumption seems
nontenable to me. On the other hand, if the conclusion is seen to be
"something needs to be done to help save the starving children," then
the emotional picture and accompanying details seem very much relevant. The problem with the argument then becomes getting from "something should be done" to "you should contribute money." That is a difficult argument to make; it may even be inherently fallacious, but if it is
so, it is not a fallacious appeal to my pity.

In actuality, these advertisements present many more sophisticated arguments than I have suggested. The picture nearly always shows

a starving child, not a starving adult, for example. That is partly because we are more likely to be emotionally moved by children, I suspect. But it also becomes part of the relevant data. Children are innocent; they did not bring this on themselves. And being young, they can perhaps be educated to break the cycle of poverty in a way adults cannot.

Students sometimes fall into this fallacy in their own writing when they present an instance of someone who has been mistreated or victimized. Normally, if they understand the distinction I have made above, they will have little trouble in modifying their thesis to fit the material presented, so that they will appeal to the reader's pity in a way that cannot be fairly judged fallacious.

9. *Argumentum ad Hominem*

It means argument against the man (and in our world, the phrase should perhaps be changed to *argumentum ad personam*). It is traditionally defined as arguing against the presenter of an argument rather than against the argument he or she presents. It seems to be human nature to argue thus. We see it when even the youngest children argue, and we see it often in political debate of all sorts.

As with the previous fallacies, there are several sorts of *ad hominem* fallacies, and there are times when what looks like the fallacy probably isn't.

It is crucial to note, first, that the *ad hominem* is a refutative fallacy. In order for it to occur, there must first have been an argument presented by person or group A. Then, when B responds with a discussion of the person or group, rather than with a discussion of the argument A presented, B *may* be guilty of the *ad hominem*. If the argument being examined is not refutation, but an initial argument about the person or group, it cannot be an *ad hominem,* even though it is clearly an argument against the person (it might be simple name-calling, however).

And it's important to stress that whenever an onlooking audience is involved, such as in political debate or a court of law, the *ad hominem* is an extremely effective argument. Audiences *respond* to such scoring of points against the opponent, even though the argument supposedly in question remains untouched. Since we know that ethos is an important part of rhetorical effectiveness, this should not be surprising. The *ad hominem,* even though fallacious, at least serves to harm the opponent's ethos.

The major type of *ad hominem* response is called an *abusive ad hominem.* In the paradigm instance, Cardius presents an argument, and

Paulus in response, instead of dealing with the argument, attacks Cardius. Suppose Ted Kennedy were arguing for some political position, such as arms reductions or increased welfare benefits. And suppose that someone answering him in front of a group responded, "Are you going to side with a man who divorced his wife, drove an automobile in which another young woman drowned, and then did not even report the accident until the next day?" If the respondent has judged the audience's character carefully, he or she may have scored points effectively by bringing up past scandal. But whether Kennedy had been involved with a scandal in the past obviously has no bearing on whether he has argued soundly for the program supposedly at issue.

The second type of *ad hominem* response is called the *circumstantial ad hominem.* It has a similar construction. One person gives an argument: in this case, let us say, a Catholic presents the argument that abortion is murder and thus must be outlawed. A respondent might answer by alluding to the *circumstance* that the arguer is a Catholic, so, of course, she opposes abortion. Again, for certain audiences, especially if the response is dressed up rhetorically, the response might be effective. Of course, the soundness of the argument that "because abortion is murder it should be outlawed" does not depend on who makes the argument. And the respondent, by calling attention to the arguer's circumstances, avoids dealing with the argument presented. A similar situation exists when one rejects as unsound an argument that cigarette smoking is not dangerous because the argument is put forth by the Tobacco Institute of America. Granted, the group has a vested interest in the conclusion, but their argument isn't automatically fallacious because they made it. So attacking *them* doesn't respond to the argument. A variation of this circumstantial *ad hominem* is sometimes called *damning the source* or *the genetic fallacy.* It occurs when someone points out that an idea was held by someone or some group that is in disfavor: "That is the very same view that atheists hold" or communists, or the Klan. Unless one accepts the warrant that *every* view held by atheists is wrong, then the fact that the idea is held by atheists tells us nothing about whether it is a sound idea.

The third version of the *ad hominem* response is called the *tu quoque* ("thou too"). Some analysts distinguish it as separate from the *ad hominem,* but it is more easily seen as a third variation. If Cardius argues that, say, one should save money on a regular basis and Paulus responds, "You can't make that argument because you don't save your money," Paulus has responded with a fallacious argument—a psychologically effective one. Cardius may have made a very good argument for saving money, even though he feels his own situation is different or that he is compulsively unable to act on the argument he knows to be a good one. Nevertheless, we tend to believe that there is something wrong when one does not practice what she preaches, so the *tu quoque* response often works. It's hard for doctors who smoke or are overweight to preach not smoking and careful diet to their patients.

The last important point to be made is that "attacks on the person" are frequently not fallacious at all. The same sort of analysis used about the *ad misericordiam* fallacy applies here. When an attack on the person is relevant to the conclusion being drawn, then such attacks are not fallacious. And in many everyday situations, the person is indeed the point at issue. In a court of law, criticisms of the veracity of a witness are obviously relevant; often, so are criticisms of the character of the defendant. In political campaigns, frequently the character of those seeking election is clearly relevant to whether the voters want to be represented by them. Within business, industry, and education, criticisms of the person are obviously relevant when evaluation or promotion is the issue. And, as I discussed above, when a person is being cited as an expert, certain criticisms of the person are definitely not fallacious.

Students who learn simply that "an attack on the person is fallacious" are being done a disservice. It is more complicated, but one must learn to distinguish a relevant attack on the person from an irrelevant one. Sometimes the line is very difficult to draw. Is sexual behavior relevant to whether a politician should be elected? Or to whether a teacher should be rehired? It's easy to imagine cases in which this would seem to be so, for instance, a case in which the individual in question had been fired from a previous job because of sexual harassment of people working for him or her.

All of the fallacies discussed so far, and some to be discussed below, are sometimes grouped under the general heading "fallacies of relevance" because in one way or another, for any of them to be *formally* valid would require an unstated warrant relating two matters that are not relevant to each other. Books that distinguish a group of fallacies of relevance often separate them from a group of "fallacies of ambiguity," fallacies which depend on switching meanings of words or on syntactic confusion. This tradition comes all the way from Aristotle's *On Sophistical Refutations*, the first existent list of fallacies, thirteen of them. Out of allegiance to tradition, current logic books preserve many of them, such as amphiboly and accent (see Copi and Cohen 143–55). But the examples usually seem so farfetched as to be completely unconvincing. Since I have almost never come across one of the so-called fallacies of ambiguity—except in punning jokes—I have chosen not to discuss them here. They just aren't part of everyday argumentation that anyone needs to be told to guard against.

I want to turn now to three fallacies which tend to show up in student writing, especially when some sort of research paper has been called for. (The *argumentum ad verecundiam* could have been included here.)

10. The Straw Man

The straw man fallacy is committed when an arguer presents the views of those who disagree in order to refute the views *and*, in doing so, presents a weaker version of the case than the opponents would make in order to make the refutation easier. Like the *ad hominem*, this fallacy occurs only in a refutative context. I take it as a given that, when students deal with contingent topics, part of their responsibility is to acknowledge the alternative views and explain why, *after examining the relevant information*, they hold the one they do. The fallacy's name is a metaphor drawn from the way the opposition argument is presented. Instead of being presented in its full living form, it is presented as a spineless dummy that can easily be burned up or knocked over.

Munson elaborates usefully on the implications of the metaphor:

> The Straw Man is a weak and insubstantial creature. He is unable to bear the slightest load. He falls with the softest touch, and even a puff of breath will send him tumbling. Strangely enough, it's because of his frailties and failings that the Straw Man is so much in demand. He is often assigned the role of standing in for stronger and better arguments by those who oppose them. He gets the stuffings knocked out of him. . . . (289–90)

We see a good many uses of the straw man in political debates in which candidates attribute positions to their opponents which are, at least, much oversimplified and, at worst, false. The same sort of oversimplification occurs frequently whenever forces line up pro and con over issues of national or local controversy, such as the current battles over abortion, gun control, the U.S.'s role in Africa or Bosnia, the deficit, tax reform. And the straw man also shows up in scholarly arguments in English studies, in which a standard opening move is to lay out a scholarly view the author wishes to attack, not always in its full context. Sometimes I wonder if we reformers in the teaching of composition, who frequently attack the "current-traditional paradigm," including the five-paragraph essay and the EDNA classification of discourse modes, have not created a straw composition teacher to criticize.

In an excellent discussion of this fallacy, Munson points out that it can occur in two major ways (289–92). One is to summarize the opponents' argument and, in doing so, to simplify and distort it, an error of commission related to the fallacy of ignoring context (see below). The second is to quote an opponent's argument directly (or, at least, to paraphrase it accurately) but to choose a weak presentation, an error of omission which links this fallacy to Kahane's master fallacy of ignoring other relevant materials. Since, on all sides of most controversial issues, there will be strong and thoughtful arguers as well as weaker and less rational ones, it is usually simple to find a weak and easily refuted presentation of the opposing view and then to claim or at least imply that this is *the* opposing view and it has been refuted. (Such an argument also involves a hasty generalization that the opponents as a group hold the view as given in the weak presentation. Such is the nature of substantive fallacies that the same argument can frequently be analyzed as several different identifiable fallacies.)

11. Ignoring Context

Few, if any, books on logic include quoting out of context or otherwise ignoring context as a fallacy. And it is certainly true that, by itself, quoting a source without due attention to the context is not a fallacy. If one posted on a bulletin board, "I cannot but conclude the bulk of your natives to be the most pernicious race of little odious vermin that nature ever suffered to crawl upon the surface of the earth," one would not have a fallacy. On the other hand, the quotation—though provocative—would make little sense. A reader would not (except from outside information) know that "I" is the King of Brobdingnag, that "your natives" refers to the human race as illustrated by European nations in the eighteenth century, or that the author is Jonathan Swift. Still, no fallacy has been committed because no argument has been made.

But we do not usually cite quotations or facts without putting them in a context of our own. And if they are cited either as part of our own argument or for the purposes of setting forth a position we wish to attack, then quoting out of context becomes fallacious. It illustrates the third of Kahane's master fallacies, ignoring other relevant data. The quotation above, for example, has sometimes been used as a premise for the argument that Swift was a misanthrope who hated the human race. I believe the quotation is relevant to such a conclusion, but in order to be used as part of a good argument, one would have to acknowledge that it is not spoken by Swift but by one of his characters, that the speaker has no direct knowledge of the humans he is judging but is basing his conclusion purely on what he has been told by another character who is often not trustworthy, and that the exchange occurs within the fictive premise of a work of complex and frequently ironic satire. Students who would quote such a passage baldly as proof of Swift's view are the same ones who would find him guilty of advocating infant cannibalism after reading "A Modest Proposal."

Since, in argument, we usually quote or cite research data either as a premise for our own argument or as an outline of an argument to be criticized, there are at least two variations in the way that the quoting out of context can occur. The opponent's argument can be quoted without acknowledging limitations or exceptions that were originally part of it. In this case, we have a combination of quoting out of context with the creation of a straw man. Or the material may be cited as a premise, either factual or authoritative, for our own argument. Obviously, if the premise as cited is either missing important contextual facts or distorting what the authority said, then the argument built on the premise isn't a sound one.

I want to cite four examples, three of them lengthy, to illustrate that such inadequate argument does exist and to highlight some of the problems in judging it. Blurbing is one common form of quoting out of context. We are all familiar with the principle that from even the most critical material, one can cull phrases of great praise and claim to be "quoting" if the writer is consciously willing to misinform the reader about what was said. Suppose the original sentence, spoken by an English teacher in a classroom discussion, was, "It might even be that teaching remedial English is a useless activity because the students who profit from it would also survive a nonremedial course and the others are wasting their time and effort. It might be, but I don't believe that it is." The blurber could quote, "English is a useless activity," says English professor Johnson. Or "remedial English is a useless activity," says English professor Smith. Or "remedial English is a useless activity . . . wasting . . . time and effort." Needless to say, this is a clearly dishonest and deceptive practice. It leaves out relevant context, specifically major qualifiers, and thus distorts the view. Any argument built on it is worthless.

When someone is accused of asserting inconsistent positions, especially someone with pretensions to being intellectual, he or she might respond by quoting, "Consistency is the hobgoblin of little minds." (If he or she responds, "Very well, then, I contradict myself," there isn't much more to be said.) Now the hobgoblin quotation is taken out of context, first because the accurate quote is "a foolish consistency is the hobgoblin of little minds," which, unlike the out-of-context version, makes no claim about consistency in general but implies a distinction between foolish consistency and some other sorts and deprecates only "foolish consistency." Phrasing the quotation that way still doesn't necessarily clarify it. The question is, how much of a context is required? A complete clause, a full sentence, a paragraph, a full discourse, the body of a writer's works, the entire historical milieu?

Some would say that, in this instance at least, the paragraph is an adequate context. It is as follows:

> A foolish consistency is the hobgoblin of little minds, adored by little statesmen and philosophers and divines. With consistency a great soul has simply nothing to do. He may as well concern himself with his shadow on the wall. Speak what you think now in hard words, and tomorrow speak what tomorrow thinks in hard words again, though it contradict every thing you said today.—"Ah, so you shall be sure to be misunderstood."—Is it so bad, then, to be misunderstood? Pythagoras was misunderstood, and Socrates, and Jesus, and Luther, and Copernicus, and Galileo, and Newton, and every pure and wise spirit that ever took flesh. To be great is to be misunderstood.
>
> —Ralph Waldo Emerson ("Self-Reliance")

I'm not sure that quoting the full passage makes matters clear, but it does suggest that the simple notion of inconsistency's being acceptable is not what Emerson seems to have meant. As I read the passage, it refers to being inconsistent from one time to a later time, not being simultaneously so. That is, because a person believed in using drugs at one point in his life does not mean that later he must bind himself to that view in order to be consistent. It does not seem to me that Emerson is endorsing the notion that one can profess both X and non-X at the same moment. When one later professes non-X, he or she repudiates the earlier view. To stay with it merely because it is the earlier announced view would be "foolish consistency."

Probably others, who know Emerson better than I, would say that even this discussion is unsatisfactory and that the quotation must be seen in the context of the whole essay on "Self-Reliance" or perhaps the whole Emersonian worldview.

Earlier, I quoted Clarence Darrow, from his summation in the trial of Thomas Kidd, as an illustration of the fallacy of *ad misericordiam*. In doing so, I was following Irving Copi, who cites the passage in his *Introduction to Logic* (6th ed. 102), the standard introductory logic text used in American colleges. The passage is also quoted in Hamblin (43), who criticizes Copi's analysis somewhat, and in Barry (298–99). Copi cites the quotation accurately from Irving Stone's *Clarence Darrow for the Defense* (112). But Stone discusses the Kidd case at length, spending five pages on the summation alone, saying it "was constructed in so lucid and lyrical a literary style that it stands today, a model of organization, clarity, and force" (107). Is Copi then guilty of quoting Darrow out of Stone out of context? Perhaps not. Copi correctly says that Darrow is trying to inflame the passions of the jury rather than argue a question of fact and that that is the defining trait of the fallacy *ad misericordiam.*

Copi presumes that trials are about questions of fact: Did or did not Thomas Kidd, an officer of the Amalgamated Woodworkers Union, engage in a criminal conspiracy? Copi does not cite the nature of the acts for which Kidd was indicted, and the quotation from Darrow gives no clue. He assumes that Darrow is or should be trying to prove that Kidd did not commit the acts alleged against him and that therefore an appeal to the future of the laboring classes is an irrelevant attempt to sway the jury emotionally.

Actually, what Kidd did was lead a local chapter of his union in a strike against outrageous working conditions. He and two other officers were then charged with "conspiracy to injure the business of the Paine Lumber Company" (Stone 106) as a way of breaking the union. Many lies were told about Kidd, but there was no doubt that he had indeed led a strike, and if such actions constituted criminal conspiracy, then he was guilty. So Darrow was not arguing a simple stasis of fact. He was arguing a major issue of social policy: "Should leading a strike against a manufacturer be considered a criminal conspiracy?" Seen in that light, perhaps an appeal to a jury to understand the historic consequences of their decision is not an irrelevant appeal to pity.

Moreover, Darrow's summation occupied two full days of the trial. In it Darrow asserted explicitly that

> Whatever its form, this is not really a criminal case. It is but an episode in the great battle for human liberty, a battle which commenced when the tyranny and oppression of man first caused him to impose upon his fellows and which will not end so long as the children of one father shall be compelled to toil to support the children of another in luxury and ease. (Stone 107–8)

Now some might say that this also is an irrelevant appeal to pity, but others would say that Darrow is here making clear the conclusion he is arguing for. To assume that he is arguing about whether Kidd led a strike or some other simple factual issue is to distort his argument. Furthermore, in those two days Darrow "took the jury through the history of the conspiracy laws as they had developed from the earliest days in England and as he had painstakingly tracked it down for the Debs defense" (Stone 108). The passage Copi cites is actually the peroration to two days of argument, and it seems to me that quoting it as an illustration of *ad misericordiam* is, consequently, to quote out of context.

Finally, the following brief news report appeared in a *Time* column, October 29, 1984:

> Soon after Jeffrey Peters heard two years ago that some hunters had trapped a rare Merlin falcon, he went to Utah to pick it up. Peters, a Columbia, Mo., high school biology teacher and Cub Scout leader, is an internationally respected researcher whose specialty is birds of prey. But he did not obtain a permit from the U.S. Fish and Wildlife Service to transport the rare bird over state lines. As a result, he was snared in an undercover sting operation aimed at poachers who illegally supply falconers in the Middle East, where the ancient sport of hunting with trained raptors is still popular and a perfect live bird can sell for thousands of dollars.
>
> Peters arrived at the federal prison camp in Leavenworth, Kans., last Monday to begin serving an 18-month sentence. Had he killed a falcon, rather than pursued his studies on how best to preserve the birds, he would have faced lesser penalties. Peters, who is filing for a reduced sentence, says he will study the work of other raptor experts while confined in Leavenworth, which happens to be where the famous Birdman of Alcatraz, Robert Stroud, first began assembling his aviary in 1920 and wrote his digest on the diseases of birds. ("Birdman" 41)

Now, in one sense, this is just a news report. Certain events have occurred. Readers must trust that they have been reported accurately. But a news report is not, in our general usage, an argument and hence cannot be fallacious, even though it can be inaccurate. On the other hand, this is hardly a mere objective report of facts. Otherwise, why mention that he is a Cub Scout leader or that he was "snared" in a law enforcement operation designed to catch a different sort of person?

Columnist James J. Kilpatrick wrote about the article a month and a half later ("An Essential Lesson for Every Newsroom"). He summarizes the two paragraphs and then his reaction—which I take to reflect the real and argumentative intent of the *Time* piece:

> The poor young teacher! The hanging judge! What a cruel and unwarranted sentence! To put a Cub Scout leader in prison for 18 months, just because he transported a bird across a state line without a permit, appeared to smack of bureaucracy at its worst. The

> Peters case struck me as a splendid example of what ails our sys-
> tem of criminal justice, in which burglars go free while a wildlife
> conservationist goes to prison. A column of outrage began to take
> shape in my mind. (A31)

But Kilpatrick decided to check with the Department of Justice about
the facts of the case, and in doing so, he learned several details that the
Time account neglected to mention. Peters was not found guilty by a
judge. He pled guilty, and his admission was part of a plea bargain. He
pled guilty to the charges and agreed to testify about other falconry
cases he knew of and to surrender all his permits to breed falcons. In
return, the government agreed to drop prosecution of nine other related
charges. At the time he plea-bargained for a one-year sentence, he was
already on probation from a six-month sentence for a previous falconry
offense: "The court revoked his probation and gave him the whole 18
months in prison."

Kilpatrick sums up the facts: "In brief, Peters was not exactly the
blue-eyed innocent of Time's [*sic*] bleeding-heart account. Reportedly
he is an able and dedicated teacher, but this was his second offense under federal laws that were well known to him." And the columnist draws
a moral: "I would hang it large upon the wall of every newsroom in the
land: *Audi alteram partem!* Hear the other side!"

In the large view, a failure to hear the other side in a controversy
is to commit Kahane's third master fallacy of ignoring relevant premises
and to commit the specific fallacy of ignoring context.

Conclusion

Some final cautions about what I have called *substantive fallacies* and
about textbook presentations of them. Whether a given argument is sub-
stantively fallacious is itself a matter of argument. If you claim that a
generalization is too hasty to be sound, remember that even a single
example is evidence of a sort for a claim (it's better than nothing). The
question is, how sound is the argument from a single example or from
only a few examples, and it's your job as the one who is alleging the
fallacy to support your own claim. Sometimes it is hopelessly weak (that
is, fallacious). At other times, it may be quite a good argument. As
Aristotle pointed out, the example is the rhetorical equivalent of empirical induction, and, presumably, he did not mean that all arguments
from examples were fallacious. The same point can be made about many
of the other substantive fallacies. In fact, Richard Burke has made it well:

> It is a striking fact that many of the "informal fallacies" in the logic textbooks—*ad verecundiam, ad populum, ad hominem, ad ignorantiam,* "straw man"—appear also in *rhetoric* textbooks ever since Aristotle's among the "good" arguments, which *should* persuade the average audience. (18)

In this chapter, I have tried to distinguish some of the conditions under which the arguments seem most clearly fallacious. By implication, I hope I have hinted at some of the times when they are not.

This chapter has illustrated some of the difficulties in classifying and defining substantive fallacies, and, thus, some of the problems inherent in textbooks which give brief lists with brief discussions and then ask students to identify fallacious reasoning and to avoid it in their own writing. After studying the issue, Maurice Finocchiaro concluded,

> In summary, textbook accounts of fallacies are basically misconceived, partly because their concept of fallacy is internally incoherent, partly because the various alleged fallacious practices have not been shown to be fallacies, partly because their classification of fallacies is unsatisfactory, and partly because their examples are artificial. (18)

Textbook authors, and scholars writing in journals, disagree over how valuable a knowledge of these substantive fallacies is, either to a liberal education or to the teaching of composition. My view is that they are a valuable part of a liberal education but that teaching them in writing courses is counterproductive. To give students a full enough knowledge of them to be useful takes more time than is available. If students use fallacious arguments in their writing, the chances are good that they can be dealt with intuitively through class discussion of drafts or comments from a well-informed teacher. However, composition teachers who fail to understand the fallacies are in no position to make wise curricular decisions or textbook selections. Such teachers are at the mercy of our textbooks.[12]

10 Fallacious Use of Statistics

Disraeli supposedly said, "There are lies, damn lies, and statistics." But we might borrow a perspective from the National Rifle Association and say more accurately, "Statistics don't lie, people do." Or to use an old saying quoted by Kahane, "Figures don't lie, but liars figure" (*Logic and Contemporary Rhetoric* 97). And if John Allen Paulos is correct that "innumeracy, an inability to deal comfortably with the fundamental notions of number and chance, plagues far too many otherwise knowledgeable citizens" (3), then fallacious uses of statistics are likely to be especially effective.

Whole books, good ones, have been devoted to statistical perversions that can reasonably be described as fallacious. Darrell Huff wrote *How to Lie with Statistics* (first as an article in *Harper's*, then expanded into a book), and Stephen Campbell produced *Flaws and Fallacies in Statistical Thinking*. I recommend them both as good books, readable to the intelligent layperson or English teacher. Obviously, the short discussion which follows can do no more than introduce a few of the most common and obvious perversions of statistical reasoning.

Statistics, like authorities and other references, can be taken out of context to create a misleading impression. Doing so can reasonably be called a fallacy, since the conclusion (the impression given) does not actually follow—even probably—from the premise. Consider the following piece of reasoning:

> The university at which I teach has 8,000 students, and it is situated in a town of 6,825 residents according to the last census. Perhaps another 5,000 people live in the country or smaller towns nearby. So if you were to open a bowling alley here, there would be a potential market of some 19,000 people to draw from. A bowling alley certainly ought to be profitable with that large a prospective clientele.

That sounds like pretty good reasoning. If I had the money and business expertise, I might decide to open the bowling alley, except that I also know some of the context of those statistics that has been omitted from the argument. If the argument were made by a supposed authority, we would have to conclude that he or she was not a person of good moral character or of good will toward us. He or she *has* the information. The statistics in the passage are all, in fact, reasonably accurate. But by stripping them of their context the arguer has created a very misleading impression.

Let's work through the argument carefully. It's true that the census of the town was 6,825 in 1990, the last date for which figures are available, and that the university enrollment is about 8,000. But the argument above adds figures that cannot be added. The 6,825 population figure includes a good number of the 8,000 students—apparently all those who live in dorms as well as those who live in apartments in the town. No one knows for sure how much overlap there is, but it could be as much as 3,000. In that case the total in-town potential clientele must be limited to 11,825 maximum, not the 14,825 the previous figure used.

Several pieces of relevant information are also omitted that make the figures inappropriate. While the university enrollment is 8,000, about half of those students are commuters. Either they are not in town at night, when the bowling alley would be most likely to be open, or they are in town and in class. That further reduces the possible clientele, probably down to the 6,825 population figure plus the residents of the surrounding area.

Now what about that figure? Well, obviously, it includes a number of very young children, children too young to be considered as potential customers. Let's deduct the 460 who were under five years old. And given the makeup of the town population, that 6,825 figure also includes about 1,000 who are over 65 and not likely to be patrons of a new bowling alley. Deducting the very young and the elderly leaves (perhaps) 5,365 potential patrons within the town. Of course, the people living within the surrounding area also include some elderly and some young children, so the 5,000 figure would have to be reduced as well.

At least two other pieces of relevant information have been omitted from the argument—although they are not specifically statistical. First, while there is no commercial bowling alley in the town, the argument fails to mention that the university has its own bowling alley. Classes are taught there, and all students, staff, and family of staff can bowl there at low rates. Since the university is the largest employer in the town, a large number of the citizens are either staff members or family of staff members. Many of the high school-age students, who might be interested in bowling, are children of university staff members and thus can already bowl at low rates. Second, many of the people who live in the surrounding geographical area are actually quite close to the county seat, a town of 20,000 which already has a bowling alley. Thus at least some of these people do not constitute an untapped group of patrons. When all is said and done, the argument for opening a new bowling alley in Commerce, Texas, doesn't look so good.

Probably the most useful advice I have ever heard about dealing with statistical reasoning of this sort is to step back and ask of the figures, "Wait a minute. Do they tell us what we really want to know?" What an investor thinking of putting in a bowling alley wants to know is how many total people might be likely to patronize the new business, not how many people live in this area.

One has to have a healthy skepticism about figures in general. We tend, for example, to accept such figures as the census count of 6,825, or the monthly unemployment rate, or the rate of violent crime. But a second important question is to ask just how were these figures assembled. Without question, 6,825 was the figure given in the 1990 census. You can look it up. But whether it actually represents the number of people living in the town depends on how accurate you believe the counting procedures used by the census bureau were. And, of course, that figure is now four years out of date. As I write this, it is July of 1994, and much may have changed in the intervening years. Unemployment statistics for the U.S. are reported each month, but there are at least two different ways of preparing them, one based on the number of people filing for unemployment benefits, the other based on employer records. And those who have followed the controversy over illiteracy in the U.S. will know that estimates of the number of illiterate adults range all over the place, depending on what criterion of literacy is used and how the data using that criterion are gathered.

A second fallacious misuse of statistics might be called the use of the misleading average. Now it is traditional in discussions of substantive fallacies to point out that *average* can refer to

- the arithmetic mean of a group of figures (that is their sum divided by the number of figures added); or
- to the median (that figure which half of the figures are above and half below); or
- the mode (the figure from a group which is most common in the group).

Let's assume a class of ten students and a test with 150 possible points on which the following scores were earned: 150, 146, 100, 98, 96, 96, 88, 85, 82, 80. For this group, the arithmetic mean is 102.1. On the other hand, the median is 96, and so is the mode. These figures are not so far apart, but one can see the effect on the arithmetic mean of having two exceptionally high scores. Consider the mean income of a city block if the landlord makes $120,000 and rents to four other people, each of whom makes $20,000. The mean or average income for the block is $40,000, which is twice what most people there earn. It is also twice the median and mode. Notice that in the example of the class test scores, 80 percent of the class scored below the "average."

Books frequently caution that all three of these "measures of central tendency" are called averages so that when we read an "average," we must be careful about which it is. Actually, I have never seen that sort of semantic confusion. When the "average" is reported, the text refers to the arithmetic mean. Whenever a median or modal figure is used, it is identified as such. The reader, of course, must understand the significant differences. Arithmetic means are the most common and frequently the easiest to calculate, but they are easily skewed by one or two very high or very low pieces of data. Modes are almost useless.

In *Hard Times*, Dickens satirized what he saw as the inadequacies of the Utilitarians' statistical approach to life. The hard schoolmaster, M'Choakumchild, cross-examines Dickens's young heroine, Sissy Jupe. He asks, "Now, this schoolroom is a Nation. And in this nation there are fifty millions of money. Isn't this a prosperous nation? Girl number twenty, isn't this a prosperous nation, and ain't you in a thriving state?" (55). Without having actually cited an average, the schoolmaster has committed the fallacy of misused statistics by implying that since the total wealth of the nation is fifty millions (he doesn't say of what), the nation is wealthy *and each citizen in it is "in a thriving state."* Sissy Jupe has the kind of natural goodness and common sense that Dickens prizes, but that doesn't stand her well in such a school, as she later recounts to her friend Louisa: "Miss Louisa, I said I didn't know. I thought I couldn't know whether it was a prosperous nation or not, and whether I was in a thriving state or not, unless I knew who had got the money, and whether any of it was mine" (55). The average (and the total) are gross measures of central tendency, but what Sissy in her own intuitive way is calling for is some information about the dispersion of the data. If one member of the group has all fifty million whatevers and the others have none, then the others "ain't" in a thriving state.

Percentages seem to be one of the most troublesome sorts of statistics for most people; I presume because they rest on mathematical calculations involving relatively complex fractions, calculations that most people have never mastered well enough to feel comfortable with them. And they are used commonly enough in deceptive ways in arguments to warrant a fallacy of misleading percentages. Several years ago, Commerce faced an election that would have outlawed the sale of alcoholic beverages. There was quite a campaign of argument, some would say propaganda, from both wets and drys. The drys published a piece in the local paper which referred to the experiences of another town in the region, a town that had voted dry. According to the ad, after the other town voted dry, traffic arrests decreased 229 percent. I mentioned the figure to a number of people. Most of them found it impressive. A few pointed out that it involved the *post hoc* fallacy (the arrest rate might have declined for some other reason than the election). But no one I talked to noted that it is numerically impossible for arrests to decline by 229 percent. If they declined by 100 percent, that means there were no arrests. Once the arrests have gotten down to zero, they can't go any lower. A famous auto manufacturer once advertised a car as "700% quieter." That the ad did not say "quieter than what" has been pointed out. But it doesn't matter; 100 percent quieter than anything else would mean absolute silence.

I called the 229 percent figure to the attention of the people who published the ad. They later said they were sorry—the figure really should have been 22.9 percent, not nearly so impressive.

In the same ad, the drys noted that the city receives sales tax revenues of one cent for every $1.00 of merchandise sold and then said that even if liquor sales totaled $21,000,000 in a year, the tax revenue thus generated would pay for only the cost of one police officer and a vehicle for twenty-four hours. But if one understood percentages, he or she could quickly see that 1 percent of $21,000,000 is $210,000. Surely it doesn't cost over $200,000 to pay a police officer and secure him or her a car for a day. I checked the city budget and estimated that the sum would pay for five officers and their cars for an entire year.

These are quite simple instances. However, things get more complicated when we talk about percentages of increase or decrease, especially if what we are discussing is itself a percentage. Suppose the personal property tax rate in a given township is 0.25 percent on the dollar of assessed valuation. Notice the decimal point. This is a rate of $\frac{1}{4}$ of 1 percent of the value of the property (often expressed as a rate of 25 cents per 100 dollars of assessed valuation). This means that if you own a home valued at $50,000, your taxes are 25 cents times 500 or 25 percent of 500 or $125 a year.

Now suppose the taxing authority votes to raise the rate to 0.30 percent on the dollar of assessed valuation. Your taxes are now going to be $150 a year on the same property. Some people mistakenly say that the tax rate went up 5 percent or 0.05 percent, but neither is correct because what they should be giving is a percentage of a percentage. The rate went up 5 percentage points per $100 of assessed value, but the actual rate of increase was 20 percent. (Last year you paid $125; this year $150. The increase is $25. That $25 was an extra $\frac{1}{5}$ of what you paid last year extra. And $\frac{1}{5}$ is 20 percent.)

Things are still more complicated when we get into compounding percentages or when we use percentages to discuss how well a business is doing. Nicholas Capaldi gives the following example:

> a large and important corporation that deals in retail sales has just reported its financial record for the year. The relevant, and true, figures are as follows:
>
> Earnings: (a) 1 percent of sales, *or*
> (b) 1 percent on a dollar, *or*
> (c) 12 percent on investment, *or*
> (d) $5,000,000 profit, *or*
> (e) 40 percent increase in profits over 1939, *or*
> (f) 60 percent decrease in profits over last year.
>
> All of these figures say exactly the same thing. A retail organization takes in a large gross, but actual net receipts after expenses are very small. The first two figures, (a) and (b), reflect this fact. You may begin to wonder how in the world any corporation stays in business or would want to stay in a business for such a small profit margin. The answer is that daily sales bring in a large amount of cash which can then be invested at high interest rates for the remainder of the year. We are all familiar with the fact that the larger the amount of money you can invest, the larger the percentage of the return. The same one percent may, by the end of the year, return twelve percent. By the end of the year, the actual profit in dollars may be, as in (d), $5,000,000. (34–35)

So what advice can be given? First, understand percentages before you use any of them. Second, if they are complex—such as percentages of percentages—get someone who really understands them to explain them, and trust sources who explain to you how the figures are reached. Third, as James J. Kilpatrick said, pay attention to both sides. The chances are that if one side of a controversy is misusing percentages (or any other kinds of statistics), someone holding an opposing view will analyze them for you if you just do enough research to find the analysis. Thorough research, rather than just accepting what seems to be a factual claim from a printed source, will pay off, a point that needs to be made over and over again to students doing research papers.

11 So What Makes a Good Argument?

In answer to the perennial student complaint, "I just don't know what you want," I am sometimes tempted to reply, "All I want is a good argument." But as the previous pages perhaps indicate, outside of the confines of formal logic, it isn't at all simple to tell someone what a good argument is. It isn't a formally valid argument; nor is it an argument free from fallacies; nor is it an argument that cites lots of authorities; and it is of no help to students to tell them that it shows analysis, synthesis, and critical thinking.

The best "answer" I know was provided by an informal logician, Trudy Govier, of the University of Calgary, in the course of answering the question, "Are there two sides to every question?" In her essay of the same name, Govier constructs an excellent argument that there aren't two sides to all (probably most) arguments: sometimes there is only one (credible) "side"; much more often there are multiple "sides." Consequently, the common model of "objectivity" used on many editorial pages and news shows like "The News Hour with Jim Lehrer" is misguided; having two equally biased and opposite positions presented is no guarantee of fairness or even clarity. The likely result is confusion, extremism, and finally a profound conservatism. (Since "both sides" seem to have strong arguments, we might just as well leave things as they are.)

Govier ends her article by giving a list of nine characteristics of what she calls a "fair and balanced account," which does not mean that a position isn't taken (see Govier, "Are There Two Sides" 53). These nine characteristics constitute the best description of a "good argument," within the public, civic, dialectical context I have been presuming, that I have seen. So I offer them here as a conclusion:

1. The language used is relatively neutral. (Example: a speaker opposing religion in public schools refers to religious people as believers or adherents, not as bigots or fanatics.)

Failure to follow this guideline involves one in the fallacy of *argumentum ad populum*, either by use of scare words or of glittering generalities.

2. Facts that would tend to support an interpretation or evaluation different from that of the speaker or writer are acknowl-

edged. Their apparent impact is either recognized or argued
against and accounted for. . . .

Failure here means that one is suppressing evidence, that the author's
ethos is actually weak, and that he or she is more interested in winning
than in reaching the best dialectically negotiated viewpoint.

3. The point is acknowledged where expert opinion is cited and
the relevant experts differ from each other. Either the case developed does not depend entirely on citing expert opinion or
good reasons for selecting particular experts are given. Those
experts whose views are not accepted are not attacked on irrelevant personal grounds.

Obviously, failure here involves a combination of the *argumentum ad
verecundiam* and the *argumentum ad hominem.*

4. Controversial interpretations of events or texts, explanations
for which there are plausible alternatives, disputable predictions, estimations, or value judgments are acknowledged as
such. Reasons for them are given and, where appropriate, the
impact on the analysis of making another such judgment is
recognized.

We live in a complicated world. Argumentative issues are by their nature contingent. What we seek is not "the truth," but a warranted belief
(Dewey 7).

5. The speakers or writers do not insidiously introduce their own
special point of view as being the one the audience would naturally adopt. (Example: If a feminist is speaking in favor of equal
pay for work of equal value, the speaker does not refer to the
audience as "we in the feminist movement.")

6. Sources are indicated and, where practically feasible, quoted
so that they may be checked in contexts where this is suffi-
ciently important.

Not to do so is to commit a variety of the *ad verecundiam* argument, not
to mention to plagiarize.

7. Arguments are careful and well reasoned, not fallacious.

The previous ten chapters have been devoted to what makes an argument careful and well reasoned: satisfying the STAR criteria, providing
a prima facie case for whatever stasis is being argued, being aware of
one's data, warrant, and other features of the Toulmin model.

8. Where time and space permit, alternative positions are stated,
explained, and considered. Reasons are given as to why these

positions are seen to be less satisfactory than the one advo-
cated. Alternative positions are fairly and accurately represented and described in nonprejudicial language. People holding them are described accurately, politely, and respectfully.

In dyadic communication, the arguer shows his or her own awareness
and fairness by considering alternative positions, critiquing them fairly,
not engaging in straw man attacks, and not ignoring the contexts of
argument.

9. The point is acknowledged where evidence and reasons offered are less than rationally compelling. An explanation is
given as to why the position taken nevertheless seems the most
nearly correct or appropriate in the context.

For many of the issues we must argue, there is no rationally compelling
set of arguments. As Perelman and Olbrechts-Tyteca put it, "Only the
existence of an argumentation that is neither compelling nor arbitrary
can give meaning to human freedom, a state in which a reasonable choice
can be exercised" (514).

All of this is probably too much to expect from our high school or
undergraduate writing students, but it nevertheless remains a valuable
ideal to aim for—whether in our classes or in our own scholarship. This
book has itself certainly been an argument. In it I hope I have come
close to satisfying Govier's criteria.

Appendix A: Diagraming Arguments

I n 1950, Monroe C. Beardsley, a well-known logician interested in the practical applications of his field, presented an apparently simple way to analyze an argument visually. Since then it has been included, with some modifications, in a variety of applied logic texts.

Beardsley's method has the advantage of stripping a piece of discourse of its nonargumentative elements—the digressions, repetitions, transitions, and rhetorical flourishes—so that the argument itself can be judged. Not that those other elements are unimportant; it's just that they can mask the argument itself. The system also allows you to ignore the order in which the argument has been presented, a matter of rhetoric, not logic.

The diagraming system rests primarily on two simple symbols, Arabic numbers for the propositions in the argument and arrows drawn to connect a proposition used as a premise to the proposition it supports as a conclusion.

I'll illustrate first with a very simple argument: "Charlie failed one of his high school courses this six weeks. So he will be ineligible to play or practice the next six weeks. Sorry coach." That's certainly a simple argument—some would say it isn't an argument at all. To diagram the argument, we go through the following steps:

1. First, read the entire argument and decide what the major claim is. It's the proposition that others support, but it does not support further ones in turn.

2. Then, reread the passage and put numbers at the beginning of each proposition that is part of the argument.

3. Then, make a drawing in which the numbers are put in circles and arrows are drawn from each premise downward to its conclusion. Put the major conclusion at the bottom of the diagram and use the arrows to show how the argument leads to it. (Remember that in the discourse, the major conclusion may be stated first or in the middle or anywhere. The purpose of diagraming is to let the argumentative structure of the passage emerge for examination.)

It's clear that in the sample passage above, the first sentence is a proposition, and so is the second, but the third isn't. It isn't part of the argument. So we have an argument consisting of two propositions. Obviously, one is the premise and one, the conclusion. In this case, it isn't hard to tell which is which. The second sentence begins with *so*, and words like *so, thus, therefore, consequently,* and *hence* are (often) conclusion indicators. Similarly, words like *since, because,* and *for* are (often) premise indicators. For argument analysts and students, it would be pleasant if such words always signaled conclusions and premises respectively, but the English language is more complicated than that.

Finally, the diagram for our sample passage simply looks like this:

Creating such a diagram seems like a lot of work to go through for such meager results, and for such simple arguments it is. But diagraming can sometimes be useful for more complex discourse. On the other hand, it is much more difficult to diagram complex discourse.

Before we leave the simple example, one more point and two additional diagraming symbols need to be introduced. If we think about the argument "Charlie failed one of his high school courses, so he will be ineligible to practice or play football the next six weeks," we realize that there is an unstated assumption involved, a Toulmin warrant. Such an argument would not make sense without eligibility rules of some sort. But the speaker assumes that the listener is familiar with the rules, so they do not need to be stated. Nevertheless, for the argument to make sense—that is, for the premises to have any force in getting us to accept the conclusion—the unstated premise is necessary. For analysis, it needs to be identified. Given the exact claim being made, we could phrase the unstated warrant as "In this jurisdiction, any high school student who fails one class during a six-week grading period becomes ineligible to participate on the school's athletic teams either by playing or practicing during the succeeding six weeks." (That was, until recently, the Texas no-pass, no-play rule.) In logic, arguments in which a needed premise is not stated have come to be called *enthymemes*, using a term from Aristotle but simplifying its meaning greatly.

When two or more premises are necessary to a single conclusion, we modify our diagram to indicate that fact. Different schemes are in use, including a curved bracket drawn underneath the two premises. I'm going to use a straight line drawn underneath them and a plus sign between them. And it's traditional to designate unstated premises differently from stated ones. Some diagramers use a dotted circle around the number; others use the letters of the alphabet for the unstated premises; some use both. I'm going to use letters for unstated premises. In that case, our diagram of the simple argument above ends up in its more sophisticated version, as follows:

The structure of the argument is clear now. You can evaluate it intuitively and see that if the two premises are true, then the conclusion must be the case. You can't, however, see this from the diagram. To do more than treat the argument intuitively, you have to apply some rules for syllogistic validity presented in Appendix B. If there are weaknesses in the argument, they are not in its form, but must be in the truth of the two premises. Perhaps the rule doesn't really say that failing *one* class makes the student ineligible; or maybe there is an exception for students carrying more than a full load (as of 1995, the Texas rule had an exception made for the *first* failing six-weeks' grade). Or maybe the rule requires that students not play in games but allows them to continue to practice. Or maybe the student did not actually fail the class but received a marginal grade of some sort. You will recognize that the possible problems closely relate to the classical stases: Did the student fail? Does the rule apply here? Is there some special extenuating circumstance?

Real discourse rarely involves simple arguments of the kind just discussed. It involves more complex relationships between premises and conclusions, more and vaguer unstated assumptions, and longer argumentative strings, in which conclusions to one argument are used as premises for another. When we confront such discourse, diagraming becomes more difficult but occasionally more helpful.

I want to work through two further examples to illustrate some of the ins and outs of more elaborate diagrams before ending this chapter. Let's use the opening two paragraphs of my first chapter as an illustration:

> In Erika Lindemann's *A Rhetoric for Writing Teachers*, one finds chapters entitled "What Do Teachers Need to Know about Rhetoric?" and "What Do Teachers Need to Know about Linguistics?" But there is no corresponding chapter entitled "What Do Teach-

ers Need to Know about Argument?" Argument and its companion, logic, are also missing from other similar books, including
David Foster's *A Primer for Writing Teachers;* Huff and Kline's *The
Contemporary Writing Curriculum;* and Thomas Newkirk's edited
collection, *Nuts and Bolts.* Furthermore, there is no section on argument (or logic) and composition in either of the two major bibliographical sourcebooks on composition, Tate's *Teaching Composition: Twelve Bibliographical Essays* and Moran and Lunsford's
Research in Composition and Rhetoric.

One conclusion seems obvious. A knowledge of argument/
logic and its relationship to composition is not regarded as significant for composition teachers. It isn't part of the pedagogical
paradigm of our discipline.

The first step is to read the passage, looking for the main conclusion. To me, the conclusion is the final sentence: "It isn't part of the pedagogical paradigm of our discipline." Each sentence seems to be a single
proposition, and all are part of the argument, except for the opening
sentence of the second paragraph. "One conclusion seems obvious" is a
full-sentence conclusion indicator; thus it would not get a number:

> [1] In Erika Lindemann's *A Rhetoric for Writing Teachers,* one finds
> chapters entitled "What Do Teachers Need to Know about Rheto-
> ric?" and "What Do Teachers Need to Know about Linguistics?"
> But [2] there is no corresponding chapter entitled "What Do Teach-
> ers Need to Know about Argument?" [3] Argument and its com-
> panion, logic, are also missing from other similar books, includ-
> ing David Foster's *A Primer for Writing Teachers;* Huff and Kline's
> *The Contemporary Writing Curriculum;* and Thomas Newkirk's
> edited collection, *Nuts and Bolts.* Furthermore, [4] there is no sec-
> tion on argument (or logic) and composition in either of the two
> major bibliographical sourcebooks on composition, Tate's *Teach-
> ing Composition: Twelve Bibliographical Essays* and Moran and
> Lunsford's *Research in Composition and Rhetoric.*
>
> One conclusion seems obvious. [5] A knowledge of argument/
> logic and its relationship to composition is not regarded as sig-
> nificant for composition teachers. [6] It isn't part of the pedagogi-
> cal paradigm of our discipline.

As I see it, propositions [1] and [2] work jointly, and propositions
[3] and [4] work additively with them. Together, they support an unstated intermediate generalization, something like "Major books about
teaching writing ignore logic and argumentation." Call that [A]. There
is also an unstated warrant that allows an interpretation of [A]: "Material not treated in major books on teaching writing is not regarded as
significant for composition teachers to know." Call it [B]. [A] and [B]

jointly support [5], which in turn supports [6]. So my diagram for the two paragraphs is as follows:

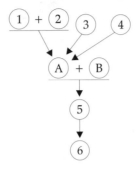

Creating such a diagram is an interpretive act, and thus complex and non-rule governed. So some analysts might disagree with my diagram. Some might say, for example, that sentence [1] really isn't part of the argument. (I wanted it to be, but maybe I didn't present it properly.) And some might say that propositions [5] and [6] are actually two ways of saying the same thing. If so, then one of them is there for rhetorical effect and isn't part of the argument. One could indicate this on the diagram by ending it with

Someone else might say the author was being ironic and meant the whole passage as a satire on books about teaching composition. The possibilities for interpretation are numerous.

Like the kernel sentences of transformational grammar, arguments can be combined in an infinite number of ways to create more and more complex extended arguments. To handle the various ways of combining propositions and kernel arguments, informal logicians elaborating on Beardsley have distinguished at least four characteristic inference patterns illustrated in diagrams (Hurley 50–51):

1. The *divergent* pattern, in which a single premise supports more than one conclusion. It would have a diagram looking like this:

2. The *convergent*, or *horizontal*, pattern, in which more than one premise is given for a single conclusion and the premises support the conclusion independently. Its diagram looks like this:

3. The *linked* pattern, in which more than one premise supports a conclusion; but they work together joined by a plus sign and underlining in the examples above:

4. The *serial*, or *vertical*, pattern, in which at least one proposition is both a conclusion to one argument and a premise for another. We saw proposition [5] acting this way above. In general a serial diagram looks like this:

It's important to emphasize that all four types can easily join together to create an infinite variety of argument patterns.

In some ways, these diagrams are similar to traditional outlines in that, frequently, main and subpoints in an outline correspond to conclusions and premises. The outline, however, is supposed to represent the rhetorical form of the discourse (that is, the order in which the reader encounters the points as well as their relationships), and since rhetorical form and argument structure are frequently different, the outline often does not accurately reflect the argument. Of course, an outline never reflects unstated premises. And usually we think of outlines as created prior to the discourse as blueprints rather than afterward as analyses.

Let's try one more example of diagraming, this time a real piece of discourse intended for public consumption, a paragraph from Gloria Steinem's *Outrageous Acts and Everyday Rebellions*. In the essay in question, Steinem has been criticizing pornography for its portrait of women. Here is the passage with the propositions marked as it seems appropriate to me. I have also put brackets around sections of the text that are not part of the argument:

> [1] Feminist groups are not arguing for censorship of pornography, [or for censorship of Nazi literature or racist propaganda of the Ku Klux Klan]. [For one thing,] [2] any societal definition of pornography in a male-dominant society [(or of racist literature in a racist society)] probably would punish the wrong people. [3] Freely chosen homosexual expression might be considered more "pornographic" than snuff movies, or [4] contraceptive courses for teenagers more "obscene" than bondage. [Furthermore,] [5] censorship in itself, even with the proper definitions, would only drive pornography into more underground activity and, [6] were it to follow the pattern of drug traffic, into even more profitability. [Most important,] [7] the First Amendment is part of a statement of individual rights against government intervention that feminism seeks to expand, not contract: for instance, a woman's right to decide whether and when to have children. [8] When we protest against pornography and educate others about it, as I am doing now, we are strengthening the First Amendment by exercising it.

This passage is considerably more complicated than my earlier illustrations, partly because propositions [7] and [8] do not seem directly connected to the argument being made. I take it as clear that proposition [1], "feminist groups are not arguing for censorship," is the major claim of this section. (It is one of those rare topic sentences that actually begins a paragraph.)

As I see it, that conclusion is supported directly by proposition [2], which asserts that censorship would censor the wrong things; by proposition [5], that censorship would merely drive pornography underground; by proposition [6], that censorship would make pornography more profitable; and by proposition [7], that feminists support guaranteed individual liberties in general. Propositions [3] and [4] provide support for the claim that the wrong things would be censored by giving two examples of the sort of things that are likely to be censored, and proposition [8] provides backing for proposition [7]. There is an unstated premise, I believe, that allows us to connect [7] and [8] to the main argument: [A] Supporting censorship would be in conflict with the general stand of supporting expanded individual rights. (There are other unstated premises as well, but in my judgment they are not problematic, so I'm not going to clutter the diagram with them. To illustrate, one such premise is "It makes no sense to support an activity that applies itself to the wrong things.") So after all that, I would diagram the passage as follows:

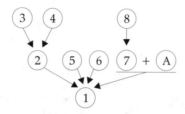

Let me repeat an important point. Since different readers interpret texts differently, there will frequently be differences between the ways in which two readers diagram a given argument. If the differences are beyond some unspecifiable line, however, there is a problem—either with the writing or with one or more of the readings. (Even that assertion raises some tricky theoretical issues about textual determinacy. Many modern literary critics would deny that alternate diagrams necessarily indicate a problem anywhere.)

The final test of whether a premise/conclusion relationship actually exists is an operational one. If you think—before or after diagraming an argument—that statement [A] is a premise for statement [B], but you aren't sure and want to check it, do the following. Form a single sentence joining both [A] and [B], connecting them in this fashion: "Because [A], therefore it follows that [B]." If that construction is not coherent, then either [A] is not a premise for [B], or the author has created a poor argument in which a statement is used as a premise for a claim that it does not in fact support.

It's a good idea after creating a circle-and-arrow diagram to take each arrow and its end circles and use this because/therefore test on them. I'm constantly amazed at the diagrams students in my logic class create; when I apply this "because/therefore" test, I often find the student has an arrow connecting two propositions that do not even have a noun or a synonym in common. The arrow says there is some sort of linkage.

Diagraming a piece of discourse is one way to clarify what is going on in it argumentatively. However, the approach discussed above does not work for texts longer than a well-developed paragraph. If you want to diagram a longer discourse, you first have to reduce the text to a set of no more than about ten to fifteen summary propositions. Then diagram your summary (see Rothbart.) Here is an illustration of a somewhat more elaborate analysis, which includes an evaluation based on the concepts introduced throughout this monograph. (This material is a minor revision of my "Critical Argument Analysis.")

By the end of 1989, critics alleged that the results of the Canadian government's 1986 employment equity program were unsatisfactory. The following text, as printed in *Informal Logic,** is an adaptation of a real contribution to the debate:

> Recent statistics suggest that Canadians don't believe in equal op-
> portunity for disabled people. Of the 14 percent of Canadians who are
> disabled but employable, 50–80 percent are unemployed. Most of these
> have short-term, low wage jobs. These statistics scare me: because of an
> auto accident, I am confined to a wheelchair.
>
> Although it is mandatory, the federal employment equity program
> has no specified benchmarks and it covers less than 5% of the workforce.
> Most other equity programs around the country are voluntary. What we
> need is effective, mandatory employment equity legislation. Employers
> must be forced to hire and promote people regardless of their gender,
> race or disability, and should have to meet employment targets roughly
> equal to the percentage of each disadvantaged group in the population.
> If they don't comply, they should face heavy penalties.
>
> Mandatory programs don't require reverse discrimination. I don't
> want to be hired just because I'm in a wheelchair, but I don't want to be
> rejected for that reason either. Such discrimination exists. How else do
> you explain that a 1982 study showed 97% of able-bodied university
> graduates were employed but only 75% of disabled university gradu-
> ates were employed?
>
> If there isn't explicit discrimination—like the time I was told point
> blank, "the company doesn't hire the disabled"—then, and more often,
> it is unthinking discrimination. If a building has no wheelchair access, I
> can't even make it to the interview.
>
> Despite the best intentions, voluntary employment equity programs
> haven't worked. Women, visible minorities, natives and the disabled—
> the groups supposed to benefit from these programs—have not made
> appreciable gains. But in the U.S. mandatory programs have made a big
> difference for women and minorities. So, until attitudes of discrimina-
> tion against these groups disappear, mandatory employment equity
> programs will be needed.
>
> It is true, as the critics point out, you cannot legislate changes in atti-
> tudes. But you can legislate changes in practices, and from experience
> with non-discriminatory practices, new non-discriminatory attitudes will
> emerge. For instance, there have been studies which show that employ-
> ers who have hired one disabled person are more likely to hire others.
>
> Strong employment equity programs will benefit everyone. The dis-
> advantaged will gain self-esteem and economic independence. Employ-

---

*Originally published in *Informal Logic* 13.3 (Fall 1991). Reprinted with permission.

ers will gain dedicated employees. Taxpayers will see a reduction in social services costs. Most important, the disadvantaged will gain their right to be recognized as valued members of the society. Remember this: just as I didn't ask to be hit by a drunk driver, it could happen to you.

"Employment Equity in Canada" turns on the following propositions:

1. The level of unemployment of the disabled in Canada is high.
2. Unemployment of the disabled is a social evil.
3. The unemployment results from prejudice.
4. Current federal laws and voluntary equity programs can not remove the problem.
5. An antidiscrimination law for sex, race, and condition of disability is needed.
6. Such programs work; i.e., they remove the problem.
7. Such programs do not require reverse discrimination.
8. Canada should pass a mandatory federal antidiscrimination law.

Now that the main lines of this policy argument have been reduced to that summary, they can be visualized with the following, somewhat more sophisticated, diagram:

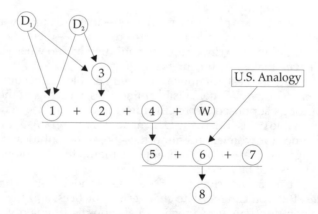

[Here D_1 and D_2 represent the two sets of statistical data, and W represents an unstated Toulmin warrant to be discussed below.]

The arguer's major claim (#8) is quite clear: Canada should adopt a form of mandatory employment equity legislation, a law that would not only force employers in the public sector to hire and promote employees "regardless of their gender, race, or disability," but also require that workforces reflect the proportions of these minorities in the Canadian population.

Subclaim (#5) is supported jointly by (#1) the high level of unemployment among the disabled, (#2) the evil of such a situation, (#4) the failure of the current law, and an unstated warrant (W) that when an evil unaddressed by current law exists in a democratic society and a national remedy exists, that remedy should usually be made law.

However, this warranting assumption has known limitations—e.g., "unless the proposed rule violates some guaranteed rights" or "unless the proposed rule causes harm to others"—limitations which allow possible exceptions to the claim drawn from the warrant. The speaker is aware of these exceptions and uses proposition #7 to counter the possible objection that such a law would enact quotas and thus violate the rights of others and lead to harming them. The arguer apparently grants to the opposition that if quotas resulted, that would be undesirable and a reason for rejecting his or her plan, but then argues that quotas will not result. Thus, *indirectly*, #7 helps support #8.

The high level of unemployment (#1) is supported by statistics, represented by D_1 and D_2. And that such programs do work (#6) is argued on the basis of an analogy with the United States. Proposition #3 can be seen either as an explanation of the condition of high unemployment or as evidence that it is indeed evil on the grounds of an unstated assumption that prejudicial hiring is evil.

But the argument has five serious weaknesses:

1. *Inadequate premises for the claim:* the speaker asserts (as clarification of the final claim) that employers should have to meet employment targets roughly equal to the percentage of each of three disadvantaged groups in the population. It is not clear that the three features to be targeted in hiring (gender, race, and disability) all identify *disadvantaged* groups since propositions [1] through [4] at best prove only prejudice against the disabled. Since no evidence about ethnic or gender job discrimination has been advanced, logically the claim cannot apply to those groups.

A charitable interpretation, however, might suggest that this text exists in a rhetorical context of ongoing dialectic; many hearers would grant either that racial and gender discrimination is extensive in Canada, or that if it were, then by analogy it should be dealt with in the same way as bias against the handicapped.

2. We have *internal contradiction and equivocation* over quotas: more important, the claim that employers should be required to ignore gender, race, and disability conflicts with the "explanation" that employers

should have to hire a percentage of each group equivalent to that group's percentage of the population. If an employer were found in violation for hiring, let us say, no women, and were ordered to comply ("forced"), then the future hires would necessarily not ignore gender and would, in fact, constitute a quota for the employer to meet before being able to hire others. "Equal opportunity" is a fine-sounding, glittering generality—but when the speaker also calls for percentage equivalents and rigorous enforcement, that necessarily leads to reverse discrimination in future hiring, at least until the acceptable percentages are met.

3. *Misuse of statistics:* two sorts of statistical information are used to show both employment prejudice against the disabled and high levels of unemployment. Without a specific definition of what "disabled" means, and without giving the source of the data, the speaker asserts that 14 percent of Canadians are "disabled but employable" but 50 percent to 80 percent of this group are unemployed. (Some of them, of course, may not be seeking employment—such as disabled college students.) The range from 50 percent to 80 percent is rather broad and might lead one to doubt the dependability of the figures, which must be estimates. One might doubt them, especially, because the following sentence seems to refer to this same group as being employed but in short-term, low-wage jobs; there is a verbal slip here somewhere. And it isn't possible to say what the real situation is without the critic's having external data on the issue. If even 50 percent of the 14 percent of disabled but employable Canadians are unemployed, it would mean that Canada has an overall unemployment rate of 7 percent just from the disabled, not to mention those out of work for other reasons, including discrimination against them because they are women or ethnic minorities. (If 80 percent of the 14 percent who are disabled are unemployed, the overall unemployment rate becomes so high as to be hard to believe for an industrialized economy not suffering from a severe depression.)

The second set of statistics is handled much worse. The 1982 data about college graduates are too old to be of much value in 1989, especially since the information comes from four years before the 1986 equity legislation was passed. In addition, the speaker commits the classic material fallacy of interpreting correlation as causation (a version of *post hoc*). He or she moves from the correlation between disabilities and lower employment rates for college graduates to the assertion that the disabled are employed at a lower rate *because* of their disabilities. But this is fallacious: the correlation would show causation by Mill's "method of agreement and difference" only if the two groups were alike in all other potentially relevant ways: e.g., in college grade averages, in distribution in various major fields, in previous job experience, in participation in campus activities, by gender, by race, etc. (By the way, if only 25 percent of disabled college grads are unemployed, while 50 percent to 80 percent of all the disabled are unemployed, this may suggest that a major reason for the unemployment is inadequate education of the disabled.)

4. Moreover, *the rhetorical question leading into this data* ("How else do you explain . . . ?") *begs the very question that needs to be dealt with*— whether other explanations exist. It attempts to shift the burden of proof to the opposition to make them supply another explanation rather than showing that only the disabilities can explain the differential.

5. Another problem is *the argument by analogy from the experiences of the United States.* The speaker asserts without proof that U.S. mandatory programs have "made a big difference" for women and minorities. Of course, that doesn't mention the disabled; but more important, the programs in the United States have often been accused of not making much of a difference, and they are not mandatory for all businesses anyway. Most important, the U.S. rules do not include "employment targets" equal to the proportion of the disadvantaged group in the population. Thus, even if the two countries are granted to be approximately analogous, the laws in the U.S. are not satisfactory precedents for the law being proposed here.

Is it a good argument? Its overall pattern conforms to those features generally taken as constituting a prima facie case for a public policy argument. That is, the speaker attempts to demonstrate that a problem exists and then calls for a law that seems to match the problem without creating serious new problems of its own. It's also a short presentation, and one can't fairly ask for elaborate and extensive statistical detail under such conditions.

A lot depends on who is being addressed and what assumptions they are willing to grant. Most audiences would probably grant that prejudice exists against the handicapped. Other things being equal, most companies would probably prefer to hire someone not in a wheelchair to someone in a wheelchair. And that makes life painful for the handicapped, as the speaker's personal experiences make dramatically evident. Most audiences would acknowledge that to be an evil.

But a skeptical audience would not accept that the problem's extent has been satisfactorily shown. More important, they could agree about the desired end and still reject mandatory federal legislation as the appropriate policy because it does seem to call for quotas and its practicality is supported only weakly by the U.S. analogy. The call for a compulsory federal law might be *effective* in an oral context because of the speaker's ethos and pathos, but the logos is still weak. Using Chaim Perelman's view that the quality of an argument can be assessed by the quality of the audience members who would find it convincing, this isn't a strong argument.

Once one is familiar with diagraming in theory, a great deal of it—especially for simple arguments—can be done mentally. Mentally or visually, diagraming has three possible uses for writing teachers. First, a teacher can use a diagram to help evaluate a student's paper or section thereof. The diagram may reveal where further evidence is needed, where a questionable premise has been assumed but not supported, even where a conclusion isn't related to the supposed premises. Once the analysis is complete, the teacher can use it as the basis for a comment to the student, either in conjunction with a grade or with directions for revision. Let me make clear that I do not advocate teaching diagraming in a writing class (although I have seen one recent textbook that actually introduces it, Cooley's *Norton Guide to Writing*). In many ways, students might be better off if they understood it, but it would take far more time than it merits.

Second, teachers can use diagraming of this sort as one revision technique for their own prose, most of which is argument, especially scholarly prose for other members of the profession and committee reports to administrators. Going through your own prose and forcing yourself to attempt to diagram the chain of your reasoning can be a salutary, if painful, experience.

And third, teachers who use any sort of prose models—either student writing or professional—can improve their understanding of the material if they diagram the piece in question. In this case, a mental diagram probably won't do. We have all had the experience of thinking we understood a piece of discourse quite well, only to have questions come up in class that we had never considered. Purely mental analysis is distant and allows a comforting haze to surround the material. Like our students, we often feel, "Oh, yes, that's clear"—until we confront the moment of truth of having to apply what we felt was perfectly clear. Diagraming a discourse on paper guarantees intimate familiarity with the path of its argument and often with the potholes as well.

I am going to close this appendix by giving you an example to work on yourself. (My suggested analysis follows below, but don't look at it.) And in choosing the example I want to sound again my earlier theme of the pervasiveness of argument in discourse. We often think of history as the narrative exposition of factual information. But, in actuality, it is almost impossible to write history as pure narrative for significant stretches of time, and if it were possible, the results would be almost unreadable. Here is a paragraph about the later stages of World War II from William Manchester's *The Glory and the Dream: A Narrative History of America, 1932–1972.* It doesn't make a very controversial point, but it is clearly an argument. Try diagraming it on paper:

> . . . The men in the badly wrapped brown uniforms [Japanese troops] were anything but inept in combat. As sharpshooters they were accurate up to a thousand yards. Each carried 400 rounds of ammunition (twice as many as an American infantryman) and five days' rations of fish and rice. They were absolutely fearless; since childhood they had been taught that there could be no greater glory than dying for the emperor. Moreover, the hardware backing them up was awesome. At Pearl they had sunk America's battlewagons, and presently Washington was learning that Nips' ships were faster, their guns bigger, their torpedoes better, and their air power matchless in number and quality. Over Hawaii they had flown four warplanes, the Kawasaki, the Mitsubishi Zero, the Nakajima B5N1, and the Mitsubishi G4M1, each of them superior to anything comparable the United States could put in the sky then. (263)

This is my suggested answer to the diagraming problem posed above. First, the passage with numbers to indicate the propositions as I see them:

> . . . [1] The men in the badly wrapped brown uniforms [Japanese troops] were anything but inept in combat. [2] As sharpshooters they were accurate up to a thousand yards. [3] Each carried 400 rounds of ammunition (twice as many as an American infantryman) and [4] five days' rations of fish and rice. [5] They were absolutely fearless; [6] since childhood they had been taught that there could be no greater glory than dying for the emperor. [7] Moreover, the hardware backing them up was awesome. [8] At Pearl they had sunk America's battlewagons, and presently [9] Washington was learning that Nips' ships were faster, [10] their guns bigger, [11] their torpedoes better, and [12] their air power matchless in number and quality. [13] Over Hawaii they had flown four warplanes, the Kawasaki, the Mitsubishi Zero, the Nakajima B5N1, and the Mitsubishi G4M1, [14] each of them superior to anything comparable the United States could put in the sky then.

I believe the real conclusion to this argument is unstated. It is something like "The Japanese military machine was outstanding." I'll call that proposition [A]. And I believe there is an unstated early proposition: "The Japanese soldiers were well equipped to stay in the field."

Call that [B]. Here is my diagram:

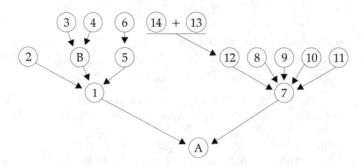

Some might say that [1] and [7] should be bracketed as both necessary to the conclusion. I would not object. And some will call [1] the conclusion and make [7] support it. That isn't a serious distortion, but the transitional "moreover" seems to me to indicate a major new section of the paragraph.[13]

Appendix B: Deduction, the Logic of the Syllogism, or Games Based on Aristotle

Although logicians concerned with deduction now deal primarily with variations of what is called *symbolic logic* (in which letters are used to represent entire assertions), classically deduction encompassed primarily the reasoning represented in the logical form called the *categorical syllogism*. As I see it, English teachers need to understand categorical syllogisms, but probably should not teach them to students in writing classes. For readers who want to understand the categorical syllogism, I'm going to explain it in some detail here. Then, I'll discuss why its relation to writing is tangential at best and why—perversely—I still claim you should know it.

The Needed Terminology

A syllogism is a logical form in which two premises are stated and a conclusion is asserted to follow necessarily from those premises. The "following necessarily" is what makes the syllogism a form of deductive reasoning.

In a categorical syllogism (arguably the major type) the two premises and the conclusion use linking verbs to relate *categories* of entities, hence the name. Here we need an example:

> All writing teachers are people who work hard for their students.
> All English teachers are also writing teachers.
> All English teachers are people who work hard for their students.

As you can see, these three propositions relate three categories, categories identified by the noun phrases "English teachers," "writing teachers," and "people who work hard for their students." Every proper categorical syllogism has exactly three such nouns/categories: they are the *terms* of the syllogism. Each term appears twice. The term that is the grammatical subject of the last proposition (the *conclusion*) is called the *minor term*, and the term that is the predicate noun of the conclusion is called the *major term*. The other term, the one that appears in both premises and thus links them together, is called the *middle term*.

The two premises are identified on the basis of the terms they contain, the one with the minor term being the *minor premise* and the one with the major term being the *major premise*. By convention, syllogisms are generally supposed to be written in what is called standard form, meaning that each proposition must be categorical (with a linking verb), that the major premise is given first, the minor premise second, and the conclusion last.

If you will look back at my example syllogism, you'll see that the minor term is "English teachers" and the major term is "people who work hard for their students." The order in which the premises appear makes no difference to whether the conclusion follows, but it does make a difference to certain standard techniques for deciding whether the conclusion follows.

Notice that we can diagram every syllogism with the circle and arrow pattern from Appendix A, and the diagrams will all be identical:

It's easy to see intuitively that accepting the two premises of my syllogism forces one to accept the conclusion as well. That means the syllogism is *valid*. Here's another one, equally valid:

All lazy people are rich people.

All English teachers are lazy people.

Therefore, all English teachers are rich people.

I didn't say that the premises or conclusion were true. I merely said they made a valid syllogism. Herein lies one of the chief problems of making meaningful connections between formal logic and composition. Logicians are little concerned (as logicians) with whether the premises and conclusion of an argument are true. They are interested in the conditions which guarantee that *if* the premises were true, then the conclusion would be true as well, that is, in the *validity* of the reasoning. But composition teachers are presumably interested in more than the validity of what students have to say; among other things, they are interested in its truth as well. Thus for composition teachers, an essay built on the syllogism about lazy people and English teachers would be of little merit (and not just because its premise insults its audience). A syllogism that is valid and has true premises is called *sound* or (sometimes) *cogent* (not *true*).

So far, I have written all the propositions in my sample syllogisms in the form "All _____ are _____." But that isn't the only form of categorical proposition. In fact, there are four forms, and to deal with syllogisms, you have to understand all four. Here they are:

(1) All _____ are _____.   Called *Universal Affirmative,* or *A.*
(2) Some _____ are _____.   Called *Particular Affirmative,* or *I.*
(3) No _____ are _____.   Called *Universal Negative,* or *E.*
(4) Some _____ are not _____. Called *Particular Negative,* or *O.*

The letters used to designate the four types of propositions come from two Latin terms, which are helpful mnemonic devices. *Affirmo* means "I affirm," and from its first two vowels (*A* and *I*) come the two letters designating affirmative propositions. *Nego* means "I deny," and from its two vowels come the letters designating the negative propositions (*E* and *O*). A proposition's being positive or negative is called its *quality,* and its being universal or particular is called its *quantity.*

A syllogism can include any of these different types in any combination. Obviously, that means a lot of different syllogistic forms are possible. The syllogisms used as illustrations so far have all been composed of *A* propositions, but we could have one composed of all *O* propositions, or two *O*'s and an *I,* and so forth. Once a syllogism is put into standard form (major premise first, followed by minor, and then conclusion), we label each proposition in order, and call the resulting three-letter designation the *mood* of the syllogism. The ones used above are all AAA syllogisms.

Several different syllogisms have three *A* propositions. In addition to the ones given above, consider the following:

All graduate students are hard workers.

All ditchdiggers are hard workers.

Therefore, all ditchdiggers are graduate students.

Obviously, that isn't valid: the truth of the two premises would not guarantee the truth of the conclusion, since both graduate students and ditchdiggers could be inside the class "hard workers" without even overlapping each other. Yet it is of mood AAA. In order to fully understand the various *forms* the categorical syllogism can have, we have to add one more consideration, namely the location of the middle term.

Since it must appear in either the subject or the predicate of both premises, we can see that there are four possibilities. Let's designate the middle term by MT and use ____/____ to represent the subject/predicate positions in the premises. Then we have the following possibilities, each of which is called a *figure* of a syllogism.

MT / ____	____ / MT	MT / ____	____ / MT
____ / MT	____ / MT	MT / ____	MT / ____
Fig. 1	**Fig. 2**	**Fig. 3**	**Fig. 4**

If we stop and do a little calculating, we can see that there are 64 different moods for categorical syllogisms (four choices for the first proposition times four choices for the second times four choices for the conclusion), and since there are four different figures for each mood, there are 256 different forms of syllogisms, each of which can be completely designated by three letters and one number, such as EAE 3, or AOA 2. A rather small proportion of the possible forms are valid. Classical logic was concerned with which ones. It would be possible to memorize all 256 and list each as valid or invalid, but that seems pretty inefficient. In the middle ages, when students worked on logic at length, the valid syllogisms were given females' names as mnemonic devices, the vowels in the name indicating the mood of the syllogism. Then the students memorized a Latin rhyming jingle to aid memory. The only name used at all widely today is *BARBARA*, for a syllogism with three *A* propositions and the middle term in figure 1.

Determining Validity

There are at least three ways to determine the validity of a given syllogism, two of which do not even involve knowing how to name its figure and mood. All three techniques give the same answer, of course, so they can be used as checks upon each other.

One technique which satisfies our intuitions about how propositions hook together involves using circle diagrams in a fashion similar to that developed by nineteenth-century mathematicians. Usually, they are called Venn diagrams after one of the persons who developed them. We let a circle stand for each of the categories referred to in a proposition or syllogism, and we draw three overlapping ones in order to analyze an entire syllogism (because of its three terms). We mark the circles in different ways, depending on what sorts of propositions we are dealing with.

To understand the technique, it's best to start with diagraming single propositions; they are done with two overlapping circles. Suppose we want a visualization of the proposition "All professors are dignified." (Technically, I can't use an adjective in the predicate of a proposition, but it's easy to see that the adjective "dignified" here designates the category "dignified people," so no harm is done in writing only the adjective as shorthand.) We first draw two circles, one overlapping the other, and we label one for each of the terms:

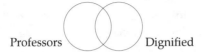

Our proposition asserts that there are no professors who are not dignified, and to indicate this, we *shade out* the section of the diagram that would enclose undignified professors, as illustrated below:

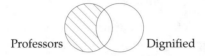

The idea of shading to indicate that nothing is there is perhaps counterintuitive, but it is necessary and it works.

If the proposition were "No professors are dignified," we would start with the same overlapping circles, but to indicate that there are no members of either category who fall in the small overlapping section, we shade it out as follows:

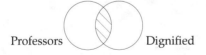

Particular propositions demand somewhat different treatment. An X is placed in whatever segment of the diagram the proposition asserts has members. "Some professors are dignified," for example, gives the following:

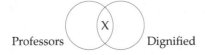

Finally, "Some professors are not dignified" gives us the following diagram, again using the X to indicate where the proposition says some members exist:

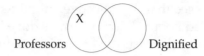

That's all well and good. But how does it help determine whether a syllogism is valid? Here's the rule: *On a diagram made of three overlapping circles, place all the information asserted by the two premises. If this information <u>includes</u> the information asserted by the conclusion, then the syllogism is valid.* Let's work through one example. We'll use a fairly complex one:

Some men are angels.

No men are mortal.

Therefore, no mortals are angels.

It's conventional to let the middle circle (going from left to right) represent the middle term, the left top circle the minor term, and the right top circle the major term. If you have one universal and one particular premise, always diagram the universal one first. So we begin by diagraming "No men are mortal" and shading out the overlapping portion of the circles representing men and mortals, for the moment paying no attention at all to the third circle. Next, we diagram "Some men are angels" by putting an X into the section that the Angels circle shares with the Men circle. Part of that section has been shaded out already, so we can't place the X there. We get the following diagram:

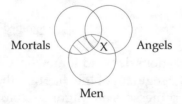

Now, to determine whether the syllogism is valid, we check to see whether we have already put on our diagram the claim made in the conclusion. To diagram "No mortals are angels," we would have had to cross out the entire section shared by the Angels circle and the Mortals circle, but we see that it is not all shaded. This means that the two premises do not force the conclusion; thus, this syllogism (IEE 3) is invalid.

Becoming confident with diagraming takes practice. After all, there are 64 different possible diagrams based on the premises alone. And some of them are tricky. For example, on occasion you need to place an X in a section that is itself divided into several sections. And it will make a difference where the X is placed. In this case, place it *on* the line to indicate that you don't know which part it may be in. If the conclusion demands that you know, then the syllogism is invalid.

The second way to determine validity, and the one most people who deal with syllogisms at all use, is to test the syllogism against a set of rules. The system is quicker than drawing diagrams, and it has the advantage of specifying what, if anything, is in error with the syllogism in addition to determining whether it is valid or not. Unfortunately, to apply the rules, you have to learn one further concept about propositions, the concept of *distribution.*

Every term in a proposition is either distributed or undistributed, depending on whether the proposition makes an assertion about the entire category designated by the term or only a portion of the category. For instance, in the A proposition, "All *zebras* are *striped*," clearly the proposition makes an assertion about the entire category "zebras," but it doesn't assert anything about the entire category "striped creatures."

Each of the four propositions has its own distribution pattern, most of which can be determined by a commonsense inspection. I'll use S to represent subject terms and P to represent predicate terms. We can create the following quick reference table:

			S	P
All S are P	Universal Affirmative	A	Distributed	Undistributed
Some S are P	Particular Affirmative	I	Undistributed	Undistributed
No S are P	Universal Negative	E	Distributed	Distributed
Some S are not P	Particular Negative	O	Undistributed	Distributed

Rules for Syllogistic Validity

1. *There must be three, and only three, terms, each appearing twice.* In one sense, this is redundant, for if there are not three terms, each appearing twice, you don't have a syllogism at all. But in practice, we sometimes forget to put a syllogism into standard form, and it *looks* like it has three terms when it doesn't. Or it looks like it has three terms, but one "term" has two quite different meanings.

2. *If either term is distributed in the conclusion, then that term must be distributed in its premise.* This simply says that if you begin with information about only part of a category, then you can't draw a deductive conclusion that refers to the entire category. Check this by marking D or U above each appearance of each term, then looking to see if there is a term distributed in the conclusion that was not distributed in the premise. If this rule is violated, you have the fallacy of the illicit minor or illicit major.

3. *The middle term must be distributed at least once.* If this is violated, you have the fallacy of the undistributed middle.

4. *The number of negative conclusions must equal the number of negative premises.* This is a classy way of summing up several rules. Since there can be, at most, one negative conclusion, this means that any syllogism with two negative premises is invalid. It also means that if the conclusion is affirmative, there can be no negative premises. And if the conclusion is negative, one of the premises—but only one—must be negative.

5. *If either premise is particular, then the conclusion must be particular.* This is a somewhat troublesome rule for some of us. In fact, it has been added to the list by modern logicians. It was not held to be a necessary trait of a valid syllogism by the Ancients. Consider the following illustration:

> All mortals are creatures that die.
>
> All unicorns are mortal.
>
> Therefore, all unicorns are creatures that die.

This is an AAA 1 syllogism, the BARBARA form we have already discussed. It is perfectly valid, and the rules above will show it so. Now to many of us, if "all unicorns are creatures that die" is a true statement, then so is "some unicorns are creatures that die." (If all teachers are hardworking, then some teachers must be hardworking.) So, if we substitute the I proposition in the conclusion of the above syllogism, many of us would say it must be valid too. As follows:

> All mortals are creatures that die.
>
> All unicorns are mortal.
>
> Therefore, some unicorns are creatures that die.

But if you apply the above rules, you see that it violates the last one. And if you diagram it with the system discussed above, you will see that the conclusion demands an X somewhere on the diagram, but the premises provide no X. Thus this syllogism is invalid. But how can weakening the conclusion (so that it is about *some* unicorns instead of all) make the syllogism invalid when it was already valid for the stronger claim about *all* unicorns?

The answer lies in what modern logicians refer to as the *claim of existence*. According to them, "All unicorns are mortal" asserts nothing about whether there are any unicorns, but it says that *if* there are any, then they are mortal. However, according to these same modern logicians, "Some unicorns are mortal" asserts that (1) there *are* some unicorns, and (2) they are mortal. So a syllogism whose conclusion asserts existence when its premises did not assert existence contains more in the conclusion than was in the premises and must therefore be invalid.

As I said, the Ancients did not reason this way. And I'm not sure we ought to either. If one is going to go around asserting that a group of entities has a certain trait, then in some sense or other that group has to exist. "All unicorns have one horn" is true, and I know it because they "exist" and can be examined in literature. I could hardly know whether they were mortal or not unless they existed in some sense. But here, I am mixing up truth with validity, and logicians would disapprove. And in mathematics, it is often important to reason about categories when one does not know whether there are any members in the group at all.

For practical purposes, some logic books omit rule five. Others discuss these problems and tell students that if a syllogism violates only rule five, they should call it "valid except under the existential assumption." Where our students' writing is concerned, we can ignore the whole issue, since they are not likely to be writing about categories they believe are nonexistent.

The third way to determine the validity of a syllogism is the easiest, but you have to carry the following chart around with you to use it (and besides, unless you understand at least one of the methods above, you have no idea why this one is possible). The following is a complete table of the valid forms of syllogisms. There are 24 of them if we ignore rule five above, and 15 (marked with asterisks) if we apply that rule. All you have to do is figure out the form of the syllogism in question and then look it up on the chart below. All of the ones on the chart are valid. The others are invalid:

Fig. 1	Fig. 2	Fig. 3	Fig. 4
AAA*	EAE*	IAI*	AEE*
EAE*	AEE*	AII*	IAI*
AII*	EIO*	OAO*	EIO*
EIO*	AOO*	EIO*	AEO
AAI	AEO	AAI	EAO
EAO	EAO	EAO	AAI

Variations from Standard Form

While the above analysis applies directly only to syllogisms stated in standard form, it can be applied quite precisely to a number of related argument forms once these are translated carefully into an equivalent syllogism. Formal logic books devote a great deal of space to techniques for doing such translations, but most of them involve only commonsense variations of the sentence structure, something that English teachers will have little trouble with.

Frequently, propositions are stated in sentence patterns other than noun + linking verb + noun. I have already mentioned that a predicate adjective, such as "red," can easily be treated by considering it equivalent to the noun "red things." Often, sentences with active verbs can be easily translated as well. "All cows eat grass" becomes "All cows are grass eaters." Sometimes two propositions seem initially not to have the same terms at all, but actually use "complementary terms," such as "athletes" and "non-athletes." One of the propositions can often be translated so that the two propositions do indeed share a term. "Only non-athletes can try out for cheerleader" becomes "No athletes are people who can try out for cheerleader."

Most of the time, when syllogistic reasoning is used in discourse, the whole syllogism is not stated. Since each of the terms in a syllogism appears twice, if two of the three propositions involved are given, a reader can usually figure out the remaining one with some ease. So instead of the standard form syllogism, what we get is a shortened version of it, such as "Since he is a freshman, George is required to take history." This truncated syllogism is what logicians mean by an *enthymeme*.

If we analyze the instance just given, we realize that the conclusion is "George is a student required to take history." So "George" is the minor term and "students required to take history" is the major term. We are given the minor premise "George is a freshman." And that tells us that the middle term is "freshmen." Now all we have to do is supply the unstated but assumed major premise relating "freshmen" and "students required to take history." Obviously, the one that will make the syllogism valid is "All freshmen are students required to take history." We always analyze the missing proposition in such a way as to make the resulting syllogism valid *if that is possible*. Since this enthymeme was presented with the syllogism's major premise missing, it is called a *first-order enthymeme*. There are also *second-order enthymemes*, missing the minor premise, and *third-order enthymemes*, in which the conclusion is left unstated.

If the conclusion of one syllogism (or enthymeme) is used as a premise in a succeeding syllogism, the resulting chain is called a *sorites.* One determines whether a sorites is valid or invalid simply by checking the validity of each of its constituent syllogisms. If you recall plane geometry proofs from high school, you have at hand good illustrations of reasoning using sometimes quite lengthy sorites almost always presented enthymematically.

Deduction and Composition

It used to be quite common, especially in composition courses emphasizing critical thinking, to teach a good deal of the above information to writing students. Most composition textbooks today either omit the subject of the syllogism entirely or treat it very briefly.

And that is probably good—for several reasons.

One is that the presentations of deductive logic in English textbooks have frequently been so confusing and, in fact, inaccurate that anyone studying them seriously—whether teacher or student—would be essentially misled. The writers of these texts, after all, are not logicians; they are former English majors who have picked up what logic they know from a variety of sources, almost never including a logic textbook. Since many composition teachers learn what they know about logic from their own textbooks, textbook errors are doubly significant.

While presentations on deductive logic have become less common and less extensive in our textbooks with the growth of the stress on writing as a process, the inaccuracy of textbook presentations has far from disappeared (see my "Technical Logic, Comp-Logic, and the Teaching of Writing" for illustrations). Thus one reason (not a very good one, I admit) for English teachers' knowing the material in the first half of this appendix is to allow them to deal with confused and confusing textbook presentations.

Although I argue that high school and college English teachers should *know* how syllogistic reasoning operates in both valid and invalid variants, I am convinced they should not teach this material to their students because it will make no significant difference in the quality of their writing, and it will take significant time and energy that can be better expended on other matters.

Now this probably sounds both contradictory and perverse: we feel almost compelled to teach something that we know well and have invested energy in learning. Why study at length something one specifically isn't to teach?

My answer is that logic is a lot like formal grammar: if you know logic (or grammar) well, then you will not only be able to cope with confused and confusing textbooks if necessary, but you will also—and this is far more important—be much better able to analyze and evaluate argumentative prose effectively. Although you should not teach the features of deductive logic to writing students, you can use what you know about deduction to help you critique both their writing and professional writing, even though you will not couch your critique in logical jargon. This, even though principles of formal logic can be applied to ordinary argument only with great caution.

Notes

1. Actually, in classical rhetoric there was a fourth stasis, which might be called a *stasis of venue*. It asked the technical question of whether the charge had been properly made and whether the court had jurisdiction. The issue is obviously still relevant in courtroom procedure, but is of little concern to composition teachers.

2. In a larger sense, writing about public issues can be seen as triadic. One arguer makes a contribution to an ongoing dialogue, not so much in hopes of convincing the opponents but to win support from the broader audience. But even in such a situation, where the opponents' voices are not immediately present, it is generally more effective to introduce them into your own argument, taking care to do so fairly.

3. Substantiation arguments are not valid or invalid. Those are traits of deduction. By definition, in fact, all arguments by generalization from a sample, by authority, by analogy, by sign are deductively invalid. (See the discussion of deductive reasoning in Appendix B.) But such arguments can be judged stronger or weaker, well substantiated or not. And at some point, when they are weak enough, we call them fallacious. (See Chapters 9 and 10 for a full discussion of fallacies.)

4. Ironically, this is the sort of reasoning we accept regularly when studies of student language skills done at one school are generalized to apply to students as a whole. The reasoning can, perhaps, be defended on the grounds that while students vary, their learning patterns are uniform. But that principle itself is problematic.

5. Argumentation and argument have both come under criticism in our era from some feminists. There are basically two lines of critique. One of them, the power critique, rejects argument because the author is attempting to persuade a reader/listener to agree. As Sally Gearhart puts it, "Any attempt to persuade is an act of violence" (195). The second critique, the cognitive/developmental, asserts that all argument is essentially agonistic and competitive and thus is suited to male models of cognition and interaction, while it disadvantages female students (see Annas, Flynn, Meisenhelder, and Foss and Griffin). As a consequence of the view, "academic discourse" is criticized for its linear, thesis-driven, hierarchical, hence patriarchal nature.

It isn't clear to me what holders of either view would say about a paper like Jonikka's. They might say that it isn't either argument or academic discourse, and is thus acceptable. Or they might say that it is an appropriately feminist argument since it doesn't seem to try to manipulate a reader, integrates the personal with the "academic," and isn't written in a standard academic pattern such as the five-paragraph essay.

While the feminist critique of argument has a number of supporters, it seems to be held by a distinct minority of feminists (see Jarratt). And even those who do hold it ironically find themselves forced to write arguments in support of the position. Obviously, I do not regard argument and argumentation as presented in this monograph as antifeminist.

6. Readers may be interested to know that Jonikka Page was an eighteen-year-old biology major when she wrote the paper. She is now completing a master's degree in English.

7. I realize that here I am ignoring the complex issue of students' cognitive developmental level. If Perry, Baxter Magolda, and a host of other researchers are essentially correct in their analyses of college students' cognitive levels, then I am asking for students to treat arguments that demand at least the Perry level of "relativism" and that of "procedural knowing" in the scale of Belenky, Clinchy, Goldberger, and Tarule.

8. Beth O'Connor, now Beth Bailey Jones, Ph.D., is coordinator of English and director of Gifted and Talented Programs at Boswell High School in Boswell, Oklahoma.

9. You are likely to come across a good many other names for fallacies, especially *non sequitur*. I have omitted any discussion of the non sequitur because it simply refers to any argument in which the conclusion fails to follow from the premises. But that is true of every fallacy, so correct use of the term non sequitur would simply be as a synonym for fallacy. When books present the non sequitur as one fallacy, they define it in a way that actually makes it a miscellaneous catchall, overlapping their other definitions.

You will also frequently come across the fallacies of *begging the question* and *arguing in a circle*. Sometimes they are presented as identical, other times as being related. The most common definition is that one somehow assumes in one of the premises exactly the claim that is supposedly being argued but disguises it in some other language.

Some of the terms for other fallacies are interestingly metaphoric: *smoke screen, poisoning the well, red herring, black/white, slippery slope,* and *damning the source.* For treatments of these and other fallacies, see David Kelley's *The Art of Reasoning* and Ralph Johnson and J. Anthony Blair's *Logical Self-Defense.*

10. All six of the "arguments ad" are treated at length (300 pages) in Walton's *The Place of Emotion in Argument.* He argues that none of the six arguments is inherently fallacious but that all are inherently weak.

11. On the need for argument by authority, as well as its dangers, see the articles by Hardwig and by Cederblom and Paulsen.

12. The study of fallacy theory is currently a thriving and contentious business, carried on in the pages of the journals *Informal Logic* and *Argumentation,* as well as in textbooks on informal logic, scholarly books, and international symposia. Even the definition of "fallacy" is hotly contested. See, for instance, Wreen, who rejects the three-part analysis made by Kahane, which was used as a ground for this chapter.

13. For a more complex illustration of a diagram for a full-length text, see my "The Toulmin Model of Argument and the Teaching of Composition" (in press). Also, see Alec Fisher's *The Logic of Real Arguments* and James B. Freeman's *Dialectics and the Macrostructure of Arguments.*

Works Cited

Adelstein, Michael E., and Jean G. Pival. *The Writing Commitment.* 5th ed. Fort Worth: Harcourt, 1993.

Annas, Pamela J. "Silences: Feminist Language Research and the Teaching of Writing." *Teaching Writing: Pedagogy, Gender, and Equity.* Ed. Cynthia L. Caywood and Gillian R. Overing. Albany: State U of New York P, 1987. 3–17.

———. "Style as Politics: A Feminist Approach to the Teaching of Writing." *College English* 47 (1985): 369–71.

Aristotle. *Aristotle's Prior and Posterior Analytics.* Ed. W. D. Rose. New York: Garland, 1980.

———. *On Sophistical Refutations.* Ed. and trans. D. J. Furley and E. S. Forster. Cambridge, MA: W. Beinemann, 1965.

Axelrod, Rise B., and Charles R. Cooper. *The St. Martin's Guide to Writing.* 3rd ed. Boston: St. Martin's, 1991.

Barnet, Sylvan, and Hugo Bedau. *Critical Thinking, Reading, and Writing: A Brief Guide to Argument.* Boston: Bedford, 1993.

Barry, Vincent. *Good Reason for Writing: A Text with Readings.* Belmont, CA: Wadsworth, 1983.

Baxter Magolda, Marcia B. *Knowing and Reasoning in College: Gender-Related Patterns in Students' Intellectual Development.* San Francisco: Jossey-Bass, 1992.

Beardsley, Monroe C. *Practical Logic.* New York: Prentice, 1950.

Belenky, Mary Field, Blythe McVicker Clinchy, Nancy Rule Goldberger, and Jill Mattuck Tarule. *Women's Ways of Knowing: The Development of Self, Voice, and Mind.* New York: Basic, 1986.

Billig, Michael. *Arguing and Thinking: A Rhetorical Approach to Social Psychology.* New York: Cambridge UP, 1987.

"The Birdman of Leavenworth." *Time* 29 Oct. 1984: 41.

Booth, Wayne C., and Marshall W. Gregory. *The Harper and Row Rhetoric: Writing as Thinking, Thinking as Writing.* 2nd ed. New York: HarperCollins, 1991.

Brand, Norman, and John O. White. *Legal Writing: The Strategy of Persuasion.* 2nd ed. Boston: St. Martin's, 1988.

Brockriede, Wayne, and Douglas Ehninger. "Toulmin on Argument: An Interpretation and Application." *Quarterly Journal of Speech* 46 (Feb. 1960): 44–53. Rpt. in *Contemporary Theories of Rhetoric: Selected Readings.* Ed. Richard L. Johannesen. New York: Harper, 1971. 241–55.

Brown, Rexford. "Evaluation and Learning." *The Teaching of Writing.* Ed. Anthony R. Petrosky and David Bartholomae. Chicago: National Society for the Study of Education, 1986. 114–30.

Burke, Richard. "A Rhetorical Conception of Rationality." *Informal Logic* 6.3 (Dec. 1984): 17–25.

Campbell, Stephen K. *Flaws and Fallacies in Statistical Thinking.* Englewood Cliffs, NJ: Prentice, 1974.

Capaldi, Nicholas. *The Art of Deception.* 2nd ed. Buffalo, NY: Prometheus, 1979.

Cederblom, Jerry, and David Paulsen. "Making Reasonable Decisions as an Amateur in a World of Experts." *Selected Issues in Logic and Communication.* Ed. Trudy Govier. Belmont, CA: Wadsworth, 1988. 138–49.

"Christian Scientists Are Cleared of Manslaughter." *New York Times* 12 Aug. 1993: A16.

Cooley, Thomas. *The Norton Guide to Writing.* New York: Norton, 1992.

Copi, Irving M. *Introduction to Logic.* 6th ed. New York: Macmillan, 1982.

Copi, Irving M., and Carl Cohen. *Introduction to Logic.* 9th ed. New York: Macmillan, 1994.

Corbett, Edward P.J. *Classical Rhetoric for the Modern Student.* 3rd ed. New York: Oxford UP, 1990.

Crusius, Timothy W. *A Teacher's Introduction to Philosophical Hermeneutics.* Urbana, IL: NCTE, 1991.

Dewey, John. *Logic: The Theory of Inquiry.* New York: Henry Holt, 1938.

Dickens, Charles. *Hard Times: For These Times.* 1854. New York: Heritage Press, 1966.

Doyle, Arthur Conan. "The Blue Carbuncle." *The Oxford Sherlock Holmes. Vol. 8: The Adventures of Sherlock Holmes.* New York: Oxford UP, 1993. 149–70.

Eckhardt, Caroline, and David Stewart, eds. *The Wiley Reader: Designs for Writing.* Brief ed. New York: Wiley, 1979.

———. "Towards a Functional Taxonomy of Composition." *College Composition and Communication* 30 (Dec. 1979): 338–42. Rpt. in *The Writing Teacher's Sourcebook.* Ed. Gary Tate and Edward P.J. Corbett. New York: Oxford, 1981. 100–06.

Eemeren, Frans H. van, and Rob Grootendorst. "Analyzing Argumentative Discourse." *Perspectives on Argumentation: Essays in Honor of Wayne Brockriede.* Ed. Robert Trapp and Janice Schuetz. Prospect Heights, IL: Waveland, 1990. 86–106.

———. *Argumentation, Communication and Fallacies: A Pragma-Dialectical Perspective.* Hillsdale, NJ: Erlbaum, 1992.

———. "Fallacies in Pragma-Dialectical Perspective." *Argumentation* 1 (1987): 283–301.

Eemeren, Frans H. van, Rob Grootendorst, J. Anthony Blair, and Charles Willard, eds. *Argumentation Illuminated.* Amsterdam: SICSAT, 1992.

Emerson, Ralph Waldo. *The Complete Works of Ralph Waldo Emerson.* Centenary ed. 12 vols. New York: AMS Press, 1979.

Fahnestock, Jeanne, and Marie Secor. *A Rhetoric of Argument.* 2nd ed. New York: McGraw, 1990.

———. "Teaching Argument: A Theory of Types." *College Composition and Communication* 34 (Feb. 1983): 20–30.

———. "Toward a Modern Version of Stasis." *Oldspeak/Newspeak Rhetorical Transformations.* Ed. Charles W. Kneupper. Arlington, TX: Rhetoric Society of America, 1985. 217–26.

Farrell, Thomas B. *Norms of Rhetorical Culture.* New Haven: Yale UP, 1993.

Finocchiaro, Maurice A. "Fallacies and the Evaluation of Reasoning." *American Philosophical Quarterly* 18.1 (Jan. 1981): 13–22.

Fischer, David Hackett. *Historians' Fallacies: Toward a Logic of Historical Thought.* New York: Harper, 1970.

Fisher, Alec. *The Logic of Real Arguments.* New York: Cambridge UP, 1988.

Fisher, Walter R., and Richard A. Filloy. "Argument in Drama and Literature: An Exploration." *Advances in Argumentation Theory and Research.* Ed. J. Robert Cox and Charles Arthur Willard. Carbondale: Southern Illinois UP and American Forensic Association, 1982. 343–62.

Flynn, Elizabeth A. "Composing as a Woman." *College Composition and Communication* 39 (Dec. 1988): 423–35.

Foss, Sonja K., and Cindy L. Griffin. "Beyond Persuasion: A Proposal for an Invitational Rhetoric." *Communication Monographs* 62 (Mar. 1995): 2–17.

Foster, David. *A Primer for Writing Teachers: Theories, Theorists, Issues, Problems.* 2nd ed. Portsmouth, NH: Boynton/Cook, 1992.

Freeman, James B. *Dialectics and the Macrostructure of Arguments: A Theory of Argument Structure.* New York: Foris, 1991.

Fulkerson, Richard. "Critical Argument Analysis: Employment Equity in Canada." *Informal Logic* 13 (Fall 1991): 171–73.

———. "Logic and Teachers of English." *Rhetoric Review* 4 (Jan. 1986): 51–57.

———. "Some Uses and Limitations of the Toulmin Model of Argument." *The Toulmin Method: Exploration and Controversy.* Ed. William E. Tanner and Betty Kay Seibt. Arlington, TX: Liberal Arts Press, 1991. 80–93.

———. "Technical Logic, Comp-Logic, and the Teaching of Writing." *College Composition and Communication* 39 (Dec. 1988): 436–52.

———. "The Toulmin Model of Argument and the Teaching of Composition." *Argument Revisited, Argument Redefined: Negotiating Meaning in the Composition Classroom.* Ed. Barbara Emmel, Paula Resch, and Deborah Tenney. Thousand Oaks, CA: Sage, 1996. [In press.]

Gage, John T. *The Shape of Reason: Argumentative Writing in College.* 2nd ed. New York: Macmillan, 1991.

Gearhart, Sally Miller. "The Womanization of Rhetoric." *Women's Studies International Quarterly* 2 (1979): 195–201.

Govier, Trudy. "Are There Two Sides to Every Question?" *Selected Issues in Logic and Communication.* Ed. Trudy Govier. Belmont, CA: Wadsworth, 1988. 43–54.

———. "Who Says There Are No Fallacies?" *Informal Logic* 5.1 (Dec. 1982): 2–9.

Graves, Harold F., and Bernard S. Oldsey. *From Fact to Judgment.* New York: Macmillan, 1957.

Hairston, Maxine. *Successful Writing.* 3rd ed. New York: Norton, 1992.

Hamblin, C. L. *Fallacies.* London: Methuen, 1970.

Hardwig, John. "Relying on Experts." *Selected Issues in Logic and Communication.* Ed. Trudy Govier. Belmont, CA: Wadsworth, 1988. 125–37.

Hart, Roderick P. "On Applying Toulmin: The Analysis of Practical Discourse." *Explorations in Rhetorical Criticism.* Ed. G. P. Mohrmann, Charles J. Stewart, and Donovan J. Ochs. University Park, PA: Pennsylvania State UP, 1973. 75–95.

Huff, Darrell. "How to Lie with Statistics." *Harper's* 201 (Aug. 1950): 97–101. Rpt. in *The Wiley Reader: Designs for Writing.* Brief ed. Ed. Caroline Eckhardt and David Stewart. New York: Wiley, 1979. 189–97.

———. *How to Lie with Statistics.* Pictures by Irving Geis. New York: Norton, 1954.

Huff, Roland, and Charles R. Kline, Jr. *The Contemporary Writing Curriculum: Rehearsing, Composing, and Valuing.* New York: Teachers College Press, 1987.

Hurley, Patrick J. *A Concise Introduction to Logic.* 2nd ed. Belmont, CA: Wadsworth, 1985.

Irmscher, William F. *Teaching Expository Writing.* New York: Holt, 1979.

Jarratt, Susan. "Feminism and Composition: The Case for Conflict." *Contending with Words: Composition and Rhetoric in a Postmodern Age.* Ed. Patricia Harkin and John Schilb. New York: MLA, 1991. 105–23.

Jason, Gary. "Are Fallacies Common? A Look at Two Debates." *Selected Issues in Logic and Communication.* Ed. Trudy Govier. Belmont, CA: Wadsworth, 1988. 20–34.

Johnson, Ralph H. "Poll-ution: Coping with Surveys and Polls." *Selected Issues in Logic and Communication.* Ed. Trudy Govier. Belmont, CA: Wadsworth, 1988. 163–77.

———. "Toulmin's Bold Experiment." *Informal Logic* 3.2 (Mar. 1981): 16–27 and 3.3 (June 1981): 13–20.

Johnson, Ralph H., and J. Anthony Blair. *Logical Self-Defense.* 2nd ed. Toronto: McGraw-Hill Ryerson, 1983.

Josephson, Barry. *Essential Principles of Torts.* Culver City, CA: Center for Creative Educational Services, 1983.

Kahane, Howard. *Logic and Contemporary Rhetoric: The Use of Reason in Everyday Life.* 5th ed. Belmont, CA: Wadsworth, 1988.

———. "The Nature and Classification of Fallacies." *Informal Logic: The First International Symposium.* Ed. J. Anthony Blair and Ralph H. Johnson. Inverness, CA: Edgepress, 1980. 31–40.

Kelley, David. *The Art of Reasoning.* New York: Norton, 1988.

Kilpatrick, James J. "An Essential Lesson for Every Newsroom." *Dallas Times Herald* 12 Dec. 1984: A31.

Kneale, William, and Martha Kneale. *The Development of Logic.* Oxford: Clarendon, 1962.

Kneupper, Charles W. "Teaching Argument: An Introduction to the Toulmin Model." *College Composition and Communication* 29 (Oct. 1978): 237–41.

Lakoff, Geórge, and Mark Johnson. *Metaphors We Live By.* Chicago: U of Chicago P, 1980.

Lee, Alfred McClung, and Elizabeth Briant Lee. *The Fine Art of Propaganda.* New York: Harcourt, 1939. Rpt. San Francisco: International Society for General Semantics, 1972.

Levin, Gerald. *Writing and Logic.* New York: Harcourt, 1982.

Lindemann, Erika. *A Rhetoric for Writing Teachers.* 2nd ed. New York: Oxford, 1987.

Locke, John. *An Essay Concerning Human Understanding.* 1690. Ed. Peter H. Nidditch. Oxford: Clarendon, 1975.

Mack, John E. *Abduction: Human Encounters with Aliens.* New York: Scribner, 1994.

Manchester, William. *The Glory and the Dream: A Narrative History of America, 1932–1972.* New York: Bantam, 1975.

Manicas, Peter T. "On Toulmin's Contribution to Logic and Argumentation." *Journal of the American Forensic Association* 3 (Sept. 1966): 83–94.

McCleary, William James. "Teaching Deductive Logic: A Test of the Toulmin and Aristotelian Models for Critical Thinking and College Composition." Diss. U of Texas at Austin, 1979.

Meisenhelder, Susan. "Redefining 'Powerful' Writing: Toward a Feminist Theory of Composition." *Journal of Thought* 20 (1985): 184–95.

Mill, John Stuart. *A System of Logic, Ratiocinative and Inductive, Being a Connected View of the Principles of Evidence, and the Methods of Science.* 5th ed. London: Parker, Son, and Bourn, 1862. [See Vol. II, Chapters 8 and 9.]

Miller, Clyde R. *How to Detect and Analyze Propaganda.* New York: Town Hall, Inc., 1939.

Monaghan, Peter. "Encounters with Aliens." *Chronicle of Higher Education* 6 July 1994: A10.

Moran, Michael G., and Ronald F. Lunsford, eds. *Research in Composition and Rhetoric: A Bibliographic Sourcebook.* Westport, CT: Greenwood, 1984.

Munson, Ronald. *The Way of Words: An Informal Logic.* Boston: Houghton, 1976.

Newkirk, Thomas, ed. *Nuts and Bolts: A Practical Guide to Teaching College Composition.* Portsmouth, NH: Boynton/Cook, 1993.

Newman, Robert P., and Dale R. Newman. *Evidence.* Boston: Houghton, 1969.

Norris, Stephen, and Ruth King. "Observation Ability: Determining and Extending Its Presence." *Informal Logic* 6.3 (Dec. 1984): 3–9.

"Oldies Outshine New Flicks." *The East Texan* 22 Feb. 1985: 4.

Olson, Gary. "Literary Theory, Philosophy of Science, and Persuasive Discourse: Thoughts from a Neo-premodernist." *Journal of Advanced Composition* 13.2 (Fall 1993): 283–309.

Orwell, George [Eric Arthur Blair]. *The Complete Works of George Orwell.* London: Secker & Warburg, 1986.

Paulos, John Allen. *Innumeracy: Mathematical Illiteracy and Its Consequences.* New York: Hill and Wang, 1988.

Perelman, Chaim, and L. Olbrechts-Tyteca. *The New Rhetoric: A Treatise on Argumentation.* Trans. John Wilkinson and Purcell Weaver. Notre Dame, IN: U of Notre Dame P, 1969.

Perry, William G., Jr., "Cognitive and Ethical Growth: The Making of Meaning." *The Modern American College.* Ed. Arthur W. Chickering. San Francisco: Jossey-Bass, 1981. 76–116.

Ramage, John D., and John C. Bean. *Writing Arguments: A Rhetoric with Readings.* 3rd ed. New York: Macmillan, 1995.

Rorabacher, Louise E., and Georgia Dunbar. *Assignments in Exposition.* 6th ed. New York: Harper, 1979.

Rothbart, Daniel. "Towards a Structural Analysis of Extended Arguments." *Informal Logic* 5.2 (June 1983): 15–19.

Rottenberg, Annette T. *The Elements of Argument: A Text and Reader.* 4th ed. Boston: Bedford, 1994.

Ruggiero, Vincent Ryan. *The Moral Imperative: An Introduction to Ethical Judgment.* 2nd ed. Palo Alto, CA: Mayfield, 1984. [See, particularly, Chapters 7, 8, and 9.]

Sanders, Alain L. "Convicted of Relying on Prayer." *Time* 16 July 1990: 52.

Scriven, Michael. *Reasoning.* New York: McGraw, 1976.

Secor, Marie. "How Common Are Fallacies?" *Informal Logic* 9.1 (Winter 1987): 41–48.

Starr, Mark. "Prayer in the Courtroom." *Newsweek* 30 April 1990: 64.

Steinem, Gloria. *Outrageous Acts and Everyday Rebellions.* New York: New American Library, 1983.

Stone, Irving. *Clarence Darrow for the Defense: A Biography.* Garden City, NY: Doubleday, Doran, 1941.

Stroud, Kandy. "Stop Pornographic Rock." *Newsweek* 6 May 1985: 15.

Swift, Jonathan. *The Prose Works of Jonathan Swift.* Ed. Herbert Davis. 16 vols. Oxford: Blackwell, 1941–1968.

Tannen, Deborah. *You Just Don't Understand: Women and Men in Conversation.* New York: Morrow, 1990.

Tate, Gary, ed. *Teaching Composition: Twelve Bibliographical Essays.* Fort Worth: Texas Christian UP, 1987.

Tibbetts, A. M. *Working Papers: A Teacher's Observations on Composition.* Glenview, IL: Scott, 1982.

Toulmin, Stephen Edelston. *The Uses of Argument.* 1st paperback ed. Cambridgeshire, England: Cambridge UP, 1964.

———. "Logic and the Criticism of Arguments." *The Rhetoric of Western Thought.* 3rd ed. Ed. James L. Golden, Goodwin F. Berquist, and William E. Coleman. Dubuque, IA: Kendall/Hunt, 1983. 391–401.

Toulmin, Stephen, Richard Rieke, and Allan Janik. *An Introduction to Reasoning.* 2nd ed. New York: Macmillan, 1984.

Trent, Jimmy D. "Toulmin's Model of an Argument: An Examination and Extension." *Quarterly Journal of Speech* 54 (Oct. 1968): 252–59.

Walton, Douglas N. *Informal Logic: A Handbook for Critical Argumentation.* New York: Cambridge UP, 1989.

———. *The Place of Emotion in Argument.* University Park: Pennsylvania State UP, 1992.

Weaver, Richard M. "Ultimate Terms in Contemporary Rhetoric." *The Ethics of Rhetoric.* Chicago: H. Regnery, 1953. 211–32.

Weddle, Perry. "Inductive, Deductive." *Informal Logic* 22 (Nov. 1979): 1–5.

Whitehead, Alfred North, and Bertrand Russell. *Principia Mathematica.* New York: Cambridge UP, 1927.

Wreen, Michael. "What Is a Fallacy?" *New Essays in Informal Logic.* Ed. Ralph H. Johnson and J. Anthony Blair. Windsor, Ontario: Informal Logic, 1994. 93–102.

Index

Author

Richard Fulkerson was born and reared in Southern Illinois, growing up in a household of argumentative educators. Dinner-table conversation concerned the political manipulations of local school boards, the merits of unionization, and the importance of school discipline and liberal education. He graduated from Southern Illinois University in 1963 with high honors as a math major, married his debate partner, and moved to Ohio State University, switching fields to English.

After receiving a doctorate for persistence, he began teaching composition and literature at East Texas State University in 1970. He intended to stay south of the Mason-Dixon line for only three years, but tenure and promotion proved seductive.

He soon moved into composition, as a member of the Freshman Composition Committee, then director of Freshman Composition, director of the NorthEast Texas Writing Project, and eventually director of English Graduate Studies, one of his three current administrative titles.

He was named Outstanding Teacher in the College of Arts and Sciences in 1980 and the university's Distinguished Professor for 1990. He has published in *The Dickensian, Studies in Short Fiction,* the *CEA Critic, Informal Logic, Rhetoric Review, College Composition and Communication,* the *Journal of Teaching Writing, The Writing Instructor,* and the *Quarterly Journal of Speech.* In 1995, he began a three-year term on the Executive Committee of the Conference on College Composition and Communication.

He and his wife, Sharon, who is director of Career Development at East Texas State, have two grown children. He is an avid tennis and racquetball player and a protesting jogger.